MAXnotes®

William Faulkner's

As I Lay Dying

Text by
Wendy Ellen Waisala
(M.A., University of Chicago)
Division of Basic Studies
Ramapo College
Mahwah, New Jersey

Illustrations by
Thomas E. Cantillon

Research & Education Association

MAXnotes® for
AS I LAY DYING

Printed in the United States of America

Library of Congress Catalog Card Number 96-67417

International Standard Book Number 0-87891-059-X

MAXnotes® is a registered trademark of
Research & Education Association, Piscataway, New Jersey 08854

What **MAXnotes**® *Will Do for You*

This book is intended to help you absorb the essential contents and features of William Faulkner's *As I Lay Dying* and to help you gain a thorough understanding of the work. The book has been designed to do this more quickly and effectively than any other study guide.

For best results, this **MAXnotes** book should be used as a companion to the actual work, not instead of it. The interaction between the two will greatly benefit you.

To help you in your studies, this book presents the most up-to-date interpretations of every section of the actual work, followed by questions and fully explained answers that will enable you to analyze the material critically. The questions also will help you to test your understanding of the work and will prepare you for discussions and exams.

Meaningful illustrations are included to further enhance your understanding and enjoyment of the literary work. The illustrations are designed to place you into the mood and spirit of the work's settings.

The **MAXnotes** also include summaries, character lists, explanations of plot, and section-by-section analyses. A biography of the author and discussion of the work's historical context will help you put this literary piece into the proper perspective of what is taking place.

The use of this study guide will save you the hours of preparation time that would ordinarily be required to arrive at a complete grasp of this work of literature. You will be well prepared for classroom discussions, homework, and exams. The guidelines that are included for writing papers and reports on various topics will prepare you for any added work which may be assigned.

The **MAXnotes** will take your grades "to the max."

Dr. Max Fogiel
Program Director

Contents

Each Unit includes List of Characters, Summary, Analysis, Study Questions and Answers, and Suggested Essay Topics.

SECTION ONE

Introduction

The Life and Work of William Faulkner

William Faulkner was born in New Albany, Mississippi on September 25, 1897. Most of his life was spent in Oxford, Mississippi, where his family moved when Faulkner was five years old. After dropping out of high school, he held a number of jobs, from bank clerk, painter, book salesman, and postmaster, all of which he performed poorly. He was chided by his father to find a job or to go to school. In 1919, preferring reading to working, he enrolled at the University of Mississippi to study literature. He remained at school for only a year. However, he continued to write. Encouraged by a friend, he eventually devoted all of his energies to writing and produced over nineteen novels, numerous short stories, poetry, and Hollywood screenplays during his lifetime. Faulkner's stories, dealing with the impact of Southern history on the present, race issues, and hope for humanity earned him the 1949 Nobel Prize for literature.

Many important writers of Faulkner's generation joined to fight World War I in Europe, even before the United States officially joined the war effort. Faulkner enlisted in the Royal Canadian Air Force. He claimed to have been wounded while on a mission. However, in later years he would admit only to having enlisted in 1918.

In the mid-1920s, he lived in New York City and New Orleans before traveling to Europe. After World War I, many of the great writers of the 1920s and 1930s visited or moved to Europe for artistic inspiration. It was in Paris, in 1926, that Faulkner learned that a New York publisher had accepted his first novel, *Soldiers' Pay*, for publication. His career as a full-time writer began.

Nearly all of Faulkner's novels and short stories are set in Yoknapatawpha County, a fictional Mississippi county created by the writer. The impact of the Civil War on the South was a major influence on Faulkner's writing. His mother introduced him to literature, and he had grown up hearing Civil War stories from his grandfather, veterans and widows, and from his family servant, Mammy Callie (Caroline Barr). Callie had been born into slavery in 1845. She told him about life in the slave quarters, the Ku Klux Klan raids on Negro communities after the war, and folktales which slaves had passed from one to another orally. He was also influenced by Romantic poetry and dark, eerie Gothic tales.

Sartoris, published in 1929, began the saga of Yoknapatawpha county which introduced the Sartoris and Snopes clans. These families would appear again and again—in major or minor roles—in Faulkner's novels and short stories. Between 1929 and 1935, Faulkner had written his best works: *The Sound and the Fury, As I Lay Dying, Light in August,* and *Absalom! Absalom!*

In *As I Lay Dying,* his characters, members of a poor white farm family of the 1920s, are inhabitants of his fictional Yoknapatawpha County, Mississippi. Faulkner's interest in history is apparent in this story, which is told by fifteen different narrators. Faulkner's characters speak in stream-of-consciousness, a literary style made famous by the Irish writer James Joyce. Characters say exactly what is on their minds, as they think it, without sorting through thoughts and organizing them into logical groups. Faulkner demonstrates how there are many ways of looking at and interpreting history. It is necessary to consider all views, to synthesize them, and to arrive at a more complete picture.

In addition to using stream-of-consciousness, Faulkner often wrote long, complicated sentences. Some of his novels contain sentences that run for pages without a paragraph break. *As I Lay Dying,* however, is different in its relatively brief narrative sections, some of which are no more than one or two sentences long.

Faulkner is considered a writer who feels religion deeply. Although his novels deal with dark themes and a number of despicable characters, he does emphasize hope. For example, in *As I Lay Dying,* although Addie Bundren can be viewed as a devilish character, she is the one who insists that actions or deeds are more important than mere words. She is a direct contrast to the self-righteous, churchgoing Cora Tull who often mouths religious ideas without having an understanding of what she is talking about, or Anse, whose real motive for burying Addie in Jefferson is hidden behind claims that he gave his sacred word that he would bury her there.

Another recurring theme in Faulkner's writing is the need for human community. If people are unable or unwilling to understand and empathize with others, there is no hope for society. In *As I Lay Dying*, Faulkner's characters, such as Darl and Addie, understand the significance of real communication with others. Dewey Dell's predicament underscores this idea: if there were only someone with whom she could speak, her burden would be lighter. Unable to open up to anyone, she is forced to "communicate" with the dumb animals in the barn.

Though his literary reputation established him as a celebrated and sought-after writer, William Faulkner personal life was unsteady. He had problems with his marriage and finances, as well as with his drinking. Despite the fact that he had been elected to the National Institute of Arts and Letters in 1939, his reading public was abandoning him. In an attempt to create security, he accepted a job as a Hollywood screenwriter. He worked for six months at a time in Hollywood, just enough time to earn enough to enable him to support himself and his family for the other six months back home in Oxford. He disliked the Hollywood lifestyle and preferred the life of the gentleman-farmer which he led back in Mississippi.

By 1945, Faulkner's reputation as a writer was in decline. His books were out of print and publishers and critics slighted his works. Only two of his seventeen novels were listed in the New York Public Library Catalogue. Faulkner was also disappointed with his screenwriting career. In an attempt to save his marriage he left Hollywood and returned to the real home he longed for, Mississippi.

When Faulkner was 46-years-old, he received a letter from Malcolm Cowley, a critic who had read his works extensively and who believed in Faulkner's talent. Cowley praised Faulkner's work and asked whether the writer would be interested in meeting with him in order to discuss his life and work for an article he wished to publish. Although he was an intensely private man who preferred to keep his private life out of the public's view, Faulkner opened up to Cowley and established a correspondence and a friendship with him. Cowley eventually edited and published a collection of Faulkner's works, *The Portable Faulkner,* reviving interest in the author. After receiving the Nobel Prize in 1950, he was again in demand for lectures, interviews, and speeches. In 1955, he was awarded the Pulitzer Prize for his novel, *A Fable.* Faulkner seemed embarrassed or uncomfortable at being the recipient of awards and honors. He declined making personal appearances to accept many of these honors and attended the Nobel Awards ceremony only at the urging of his daughter, Jill.

During the 1950s, Faulkner spoke out against racism in response to the tensions surrounding the growing Civil Rights movement. He had upset some fellow Mississippians by saying that African Americans ought to be able to attend the University of Mississippi. Though he firmly believed in racial equality, he believed that Northerners should not force integration on Southerners. As a Southerner, he insisted that Northerners could not understand the South's deeply rooted emotions concerning race relations nor could they understand the history which bound the two races together in a way which only fellow Southerners, both black and white, could appreciate. His middle-of-the-road stance was realistic. However, he was threatened and criticized by some members of both races.

Before his death, William Faulkner was working as a writer in residence at The University of Virginia and had just completed his last novel, *The Reivers,* which was scheduled for publication in June 1962. While other writers of his generation sought inspiration abroad and wrote about cosmopolitan characters engaged in universal conflicts and questions, Faulkner is remarkable for having expressed the same kinds of universal themes through characters and plots based in Southern history and a small, fictional Mississippi county. His reputation as one of America's greatest writers was secure. At the age of 65, six weeks after receiving the Gold Medal for Fiction, William Faulkner died on July 6, 1962, in Oxford, Mississippi.

Historical Background

World War I caused many social and cultural changes in the United States. The prim and proper ways of the Victorian and Edwardian world were replaced by openness about sex, more permissiveness in dating, drinking, smoking, and fewer restrictions on women's behavior. The exposure to other cultures which servicemen had experienced resulted in a greater exchange of artistic and philosophical ideas. Modern, abstract, and experimental art, poetry, music, and novel writing were introduced to America. In exchange, America gave the world jazz music. Many American writers and artists found the atmosphere in Europe to be freer and more open to new ideas. They became expatriates and spent much of their lives practicing their art abroad. This period produced some of America's best writers: F. Scott Fitzgerald, Ernest Hemingway, John Dos Passos, John Steinbeck, and William Faulkner.

Another significant by-product of the war was the changing role of African Americans. Segregated units had been sent overseas to fight. However, the European black soldiers were not met with prejudice. For the first time, especially among those black soldiers recruited from the South, they were treated as equals by white people. On returning home to America, they anticipated the same treatment but were met with increased prejudice. Lynchings, riots, and violence broke out all across the country over race issues. The war had changed the face of the world, but America was not ready for all the changes.

Technology was advancing at an astounding pace. Talking pictures were introduced in the late 1920s, the radio brought music, news, and advertising into everyone's home, and the popularity of the automobile caused the first traffic jams in history. Wartime pilots were now stunt pilots, couriers, and commercial airline entrepreneurs. Household appliances and conveniences made chores easier, provided more leisure time, and created a nation of consumers.

Golf, football, swimming, skiing, and other sports changed our attitudes about health and recreation. Young people now preferred a healthy tan to a refined pallor. The feminine standard of beauty changed from the round, soft curves and flowing hair of the Gibson girl to the thin, straight, boyish figure and short, bobbed hair of the Flapper.

Faulkner began *As I Lay Dying* during the time of the great stockmarket crash of 1929. The novel was published the following year. Though many wealthy people lost their fortunes because of the crash, the financial disaster affected every part of society. Rural and farm families, like the Bundrens of *As I Lay Dying*, lost whatever savings they might have had. Because of the poor economy, there was less demand for farm products. As the prices dropped, farmers lost the ability to upgrade their operations, buy essential supplies, and pay their existing bills. Many farmers had to sell off their livestock and equipment just to buy the necessities of life. During the Dust Bowl exodus of the 1930s, large numbers of farm families from the South, Southwest, and Midwest lost their farms and moved West in search of migratory work on California fruit and vegetable farms. John Steinbeck's classic novel, *The Grapes of Wrath*, describes how the Great Depression breaks up a close family when foreclosure forces them to move from the farm on which they had been living together for generations.

William Faulkner is one of the great writers of the "Jazz Age" of post-World War I America. He wrote *As I Lay Dying* in only six weeks while he was working the nightshift at a local powerhouse. He used the back of an old wheelbarrow for a desk and wrote between eleven at night and four in the morning. Whereas most novelists of his generation set their stories in cosmopolitan or exotic locales, *As I Lay Dying*, like most of Faulkner's stories, takes place in a small Southern community, much like the Oxford, Mississippi in which he spent most of his life. The novel depicts the difficult life of impoverished and poorly educated Southern farm families during this period.

The hardships of the Bundren family and the preoccupation of each individual with his or her own interests, needs, and desires reflect the way in which people face misfortune and disasters, each with his own agenda. Though some characters might seem less than admirable, they are realistic if we consider how we might react in their place. The novel received successful reviews and helped establish Faulkner's early reputation. It is considered among his greatest achievements.

Master List of Characters

Addie Bundren—*The dying character of the title, a former school-teacher and wife to Anse Bundren; a proud, bitter, and unhappy woman who insisted on being buried in her own family's plot in Jefferson when she died.*

Anse Bundren—*Poor white farmer, married to Addie; lazy, pathetic, and self-centered; hopes to buy false teeth for himself after they bury Addie in Jefferson.*

Cash Bundren—*The Bundren's first-born son; a skilled carpenter who has built his mother's casket; injured on the way to Jefferson.*

Darl Bundren—*Addie and Anse's second son and the main narrator of the story; considered mentally defective by others.*

Jewel Bundren—*Illegitimate son of Addie and Preacher Whitfield; Addie's third and favorite child.*

Dewey Dell Bundren—*The Bundren boys' pregnant, unwed sister, who hopes to get an abortion in Jefferson.*

Vardaman Bundren—*The youngest son of the Bundrens.*

Cora Tull—*Religious woman, neighbor to the Bundren family; always advising Addie to put her faith in God, to be religious, and to ask God for forgiveness.*

Miss Lawington—*Woman mentioned by Cora Tull; gave Cora advice about buying chickens and selling her cakes.*

Kate—*Neighbor to the Bundrens; visits Addie on her deathbed.*

Eula—*Neighbor to the Bundrens; visits Addie on her deathbed.*

Vernon Tull—*Cora's husband; He accompanies the Bundrens part of the way on their journey to Jefferson.*

Dr. Peabody—*Country doctor who attends to Addie during her illness.*

Reverend Whitfield—*Hypocritical preacher who was Addie's lover and Jewel's father; relieved to hear she has died without revealing their secret.*

Lafe—*Young male neighbor to the Bundrens; attracted to Dewey Dell.*

Suratt—*Man who owns a talking machine which Cash would like to buy.*

Quick—*He and his father sold a spotted horse to Jewel; attends Addie's funeral.*

Lon Quick—*Raises shoats and sells horses.*

Uncle Billy Varner—*Neighbor to the Bundrens.*

Jody Varner—*Mentioned as Uncle Billy's son.*

Houston—*Neighbor of the Bundrens; attends Addie's funeral.*

Littlejohn—*Neighbor of the Bundrens; attends Addie's funeral.*

MacCallum—*Neighbor of the Bundrens.*

Samson—*Neighbor of the Bundrens; lets them "store" Addie's body in his barn overnight and notices a buzzard hanging around the corpse the next morning.*

Rachel—*Samson's wife.*

Flem Snopes—*Mentioned as the man who brought some wild horses to the community.*

Snopes—*Nephew to Flem; sells mules to the Bundren family.*

Eustace Grimm—*Works for Snopes.*

Armstid—*Neighbor of the Bundrens; attends Addie's funeral; He lets the Bundrens stay in his barn when they are on their way to Jefferson.*

Lula Armstid—*Armstid's wife; Darl mentions that she offers to prepare food and lodging for the Bundren family when they prepare to spend the night.*

Moseley—*Older druggist who refuses to give Dewey Dell the medicine to terminate her pregnancy.*

Grummet—*Owner of the hardware store in Mottson.*

Albert—*Resident of Mottson; tells Moseley about the commotion the Bundren wagon caused in town.*

Marshal—*Lawman in Mottson; speaks with the Bundren family about the smell coming from the wagon.*

Mr. Gillespie—*Farmer who lets the Bundrens store Addie's casket in his barn.*

Mack Gillespie—*Gillespie's son.*

Three negroes on the road—*Notice the odor coming from the Bundren wagon.*

White man on the road—*Comments on the odor from the wagon and nearly gets into a fight with Jewel.*

Two officials—*Law officers who wrestle with Darl in order to detain him for burning the Gillespie barn.*

Skeet MacGowan—*Druggist's clerk who pretends to be a doctor; fools Dewey Dell into having sex with him in order to "reverse" her pregnancy.*

Jody—*The second Jody encountered in the novel; another druggist's clerk who works with Skeets MacGowan.*

"The old man" who owns the drugstore—*MacGowan's and Jody's boss; the druggist in Jefferson.*

Alford—*Mentioned by MacGowan; either a doctor or lawyer to whom they might send Dewey Dell.*

The new Mrs. Bundren—*A duck-shaped woman with pop-eyes who lives in Jefferson.*

Summary of the Novel

Addie Bundren, the wife and mother to a poor white farm family, is on her deathbed. Friends and family members gather around to comfort her and to prepare for her funeral. Addie, a proud and bitter woman, has no interest in the religious comfort her neighbor, Cora Tull, offers. She is tired of living, loves only her son, Jewel, and despises her husband, neighbors, and all others around her. She desires only to be buried among her own family members in the town of Jefferson. She has made her useless and ineffectual husband promise to do as she wishes and, upon her death, the family sets out for Jefferson with her corpse in a casket.

On the way to Jefferson, each member of the family narrates part of the story and relates what happens during the journey or what has happened in the past. Each of the narrators has his or her own reason for making the trip. Anse wants to get a set of false teeth. Dewey Dell, the daughter, needs an abortion. Cash plans to buy a record-player. The baby, Vardaman, is promised a toy and exotic fruit (bananas) when they get to town. The only characters who have no material stake in getting to Jefferson are Addie's sons, Darl and Jewel. Darl is as determined to prevent the grotesque affair as Jewel is to carry out his mother's wish. Darl uses every obstacle or setback to try to prevent Addie's casket from getting to Jefferson.

Many incidents occur which seemingly frustrate Addie's progress toward being buried in the soil of her home town. Her youngest son, drilling holes in her casket so she can breathe, instead, drills through to her face. The casket is overturned while the family is crossing a river and nearly gets washed away. Cash, one of Addie's sons, injures his leg and needs a doctor. However, the family refuses to postpone its journey. These setbacks make the trip longer than expected, and the body begins to decompose. Followed by cats and buzzards, and accompanied by a terrible odor, the burial procession is chased out of towns. Darl fights with his brother Jewel, who is intent on burying Addie in her family plot. When he sets fire to one of the barns holding the corpse, Jewel must "rescue" Addie.

When they reach Jefferson, Anse goes into a house to borrow spades to dig Addie's grave. His family waits in the wagon and wonders why it takes him so long. They see a woman peering out at them from behind the curtains of a window. Cash's leg becomes gangerous because of the makeshift cement cast which Anse made for him. Dewey Dell, nervous because Darl knows her secret, turns him in for burning the barn. He is arrested and taken away to the asylum for being insane. Dewey Dell is fooled by a druggist's clerk pretending to be a doctor. He gives her some talcum powder in capsules for medicine, then convinces her that she needs to have sex again in order to undo her "problem." Anse, who has sold Jewel's prized horse, stolen money Cash was planning to use for a gramophone, and wheedled Dewey Dell's ten-dollar abortion money from her, uses the funds to get a shave, haircut, and new teeth. After Addie is buried, he returns to the Jefferson house, goes inside, and brings out the new Mrs. Bundren, a flashily dressed woman, shaped like a duck, with hard-looking pop eyes who joins the family in their wagon.

Estimated Reading Time

The average reader should be able to complete the entire novel in approximately eight to ten hours.

It is recommended that the novel be divided into five sections of approximately 50 pages each. These blocks divide the story into what happens up to Addie's death, preparing to journey to Jefferson, the coffin overturning in the river, the makeshift repair of Cash's leg with cement, and the fire through meeting the new Mrs. Bundren. In this study guide, study questions and suggested essay topics follow the summary and discussion of each of the study blocks.

UNIT ONE:	Addie's Death	Reading Time: 2 hrs.
UNIT TWO:	Preparing to Journey	Reading Time: 1.50 - 2 hrs.
UNIT THREE:	Through the River	Reading Time: 1.50 - 2 hrs.
UNIT FOUR:	Cash's Leg	Reading Time: 1.50 - 2 hrs.
UNIT FIVE:	Fire to Finish	Reading Time: 1.50 - 2 hrs.

Although many events are crowded into the novel, the whole story takes place within the period of about eight or nine days. The following timeline can help in locating when major events occur during the story:

DAY ONE: Addie Bundren is on her deathbed. Her family, female neighbors, and her doctor are around her. Her eldest son, Cash, is building her casket out in the yard. Her two sons, Jewel and Darl, must leave her to go complete a job. She dies before they return. Upset by Addie's death, Vardaman, the youngest child, runs away to the neighbors' house. They bring him home and help carry the completed casket into the house.

DAY TWO: Addie is put in her casket and neighbors gather for the funeral. The preacher gives the sermon and leads the visiting neighbors and friends in the singing. Vardaman bores auger holes in the casket lid to provide air for Addie.

DAY THREE: Jewel and Darl finally return home. They load her casket onto the wagon to carry her back to her family burial ground in Jefferson. The casket breaks free of their grip and slips down the slope of their hill, upsetting the contents. The family spends the night in the barn at Samson's farm.

DAY FOUR: As the Bundrens leave his farm, Samson notices a buzzard in the barn where the casket was stored. Attempting to cross a washed out bridge, the wagon overturns. The mules are lost, Cash is injured, and the casket, which Darl has tried not to save, is drenched with water. The Bundrens spend the night at Armstid's farm. Uncle Billy tries to fix Cash's leg.

DAY FIVE: The family is still at the Armstid farm. Anse goes off on Jewel's horse to see about replacing the mules which were lost. More buzzards surround the casket. Anse uses Jewel's horse and money he has taken from Cash's pockets to negotiate a deal for new mules. Jewel, angry with Anse, rides off. The family spends another night near the Armstid farm.

DAY SIX: The Bundren's have left the Armstid farm. Cash's leg is getting worse. More buzzards follow the wagon to Mottson. In town, Dewey Dell tries to purchase abortion medicine from a druggist who angrily turns her down. The family buys cement with which they plan to set Cash's leg. The town marshal forces them to leave Mottson because of the stench from Addie's corpse. Someone in town says the person has been dead eight days. Jewel returns to join the family. They spend the night at the Gillespie farm. Darl sets fire to the barn in an attempt to burn Addie's casket.

DAY SEVEN: The family continues on their journey and finally reaches Jefferson. Dewey Dell dresses up in her Sunday best before they enter town. On the road into Jefferson, three negroes and a white man comment on the awful smell from the wagon. Jewel nearly gets into a fight with the white man. Anse pulls the wagon in front of a house from which the sounds of a gramophone can be heard. He goes inside to see if he can borrow some spades to dig Addie's grave. Officials from Jackson wrestle Darl to the ground to take him away to the asylum for burning the Gillespie barn. Dewey Dell visits the Jefferson druggist to find her medicine and the druggist's clerk convinces her that he can help her if she returns that night. When Dewey Dell comes back later, he persuades her that having sex with him will reverse her pregnancy. She has sex with the druggist, but she realizes that she has been duped. Addie is buried.

DAY EIGHT: Darl is put on the train for Jackson. Anse takes the ten dollars Dewey Dell was going to use for her medicine to get a shave and a haircut. He returns the spades to the woman from whom he borrowed them. The family goes to Peabody's and Anse goes out at night to attend to "some business."

DAY NINE: Anse goes out early in the morning. He comes back to ask his children if any of them have any more money. He tells them he must go out again and that they should all meet at the corner at a specified time. Waiting in the wagon, at the corner, they see Anse wearing his newly-purchased teeth. They are shocked when he introduces them to the new Mrs. Bundren, the woman from whom he had borrowed the spades that helped bury Addie.

Unit 1

New Characters:

Darl Bundren: *main narrator; second son of Addie and Anse Bundren*

Cora Tull: *religious neighbor of the Bundrens, at the house for Addie's "passing"*

Kate: *another neighbor and a friend of Cora Tull's*

Eula: *another visitor and friend of Cora Tull's*

Miss Lawington: *friend of Cora Tull's; Cora mentions that this woman has given her advice on what type of chickens to breed and where she might sell her cakes for pocket money*

Jewel Bundren: *Addie's third son*

Dewey Dell: *only daughter of Anse and Addie Bundren; she is quiet and sullen*

Vernon Tull: *Cora Tull's husband; closest thing to a friend the Bundrens have*

Dr. Peabody: *country doctor called in to Addie's death bed*

Vardaman Bundren: *youngest son and last Bundren child*

Cash Bundren: *first born son of Addie and Anse Bundren*

Addie Bundren: *wife and mother to the Bundren clan; she is on her deathbed having given up the desire to live*

Anse Bundren: *Addie's husband; a poor farmer who is constantly whining about his problems but who manages to get others to do all his work for him*

Lafe: *a neighbor boy who is attracted to Dewey Dell; does not have his own narrative, but is an important part of Dewey's narrative*

Summary

Brothers Jewel and Darl Bundren, who have been working together in the field, stop working and walk the path back to their house. Neither one speaks to the other. Darl describes his brother's rigid, grave, and cold demeanor. In the distance, the sound of a carpenter at work can be heard. It is their other brother, Cash, who is working on a casket for Addie Bundren. Darl tells us that Cash is a good carpenter.

Cora Tull narrates the next section. She is speaking with a woman named Kate about baking cakes for rich folks. Cora relies on God's will and wisdom and does not question His plans for people. She is watching Addie Bundren, who is wasting away before her. She notes that Addie will not have everlasting salvation and grace, though she is on her deathbed. She tells the other woman that Addie is listening to her son building her casket.

Darl sees his father, a worn-out and unkempt man, on the porch with Vernon Tull. He contrasts Anse's appearance with that of Tull, whose wife, he supposes, has some say over his dress. Darl notices Jewel calling to his horse. When it comes to him, it suddenly rears up and appears savage, terrible, and rigid. He thinks of Jewel and the horse as one figure. Jewel can control the horse, but he does it with violent gestures and curses. When he puts the horse in the stall, the horse tries to kick him, and he kicks back. Though he is very brutal with the animal, he mixes his curses with sweet words.

Jewel narrates a brief section in which he is angry at Cash for his continual sawing and hammering on the casket. He calls the others buzzards who seem to be waiting for Addie to die. He doubts the existence of God because, he says, "What the hell is He for?" Jewel imagines what it would be like if other family members had died when they had accidents. He says that there would have been no others, just he and Addie, living high on the hill. He imagines that he could protect her from the curious by throwing rocks at their faces.

Darl notes that he has never seen his father sweat. In fact, his father believes that if he ever sweats, he will die. When Darl insists that they had better go earn three dollars by finishing some job quickly, Jewel believes that their mother is not so sick that they need to rush. Anse keeps repeating how luckless he is and how terrible the situation is. He says Addie wanted to be buried in a home-built

casket and put to rest in her family plot in Jefferson. Because he promised her he would follow her wishes, he insists his sons not return late so they can get to her family plot right away.

Cora compares Darl and Jewel. She says that Anse and Jewel were more interested in making money than in saying good-bye to Addie. She believes that Darl loves his mother though Addie preferred Jewel. She mentions her own self-sacrifices in devoting the last three weeks to the Bundrens' sorrow. She doesn't believe that Addie wanted to be buried in Jefferson because she wouldn't want to be buried apart from her husband and children. She reflects on Darl standing in the doorway and staring at his dying mother. She says he couldn't speak because his heart was "too full for words."

Dewey Dell mentions that Anse is afraid to work and sweat, so he lets his neighbors do his work for him. She doesn't think Jewel feels any kinship ties with the rest of the family, and she considers Darl strange and distant. She describes a time she and Lafe, a farm hand, were picking rows of cotton. She made a deal with herself that if the sack was full by the end of the row, she would go into the woods with Lafe. She noticed that he was putting the cotton he picked into her sack so it would be full. She realizes that Darl knows what she and Lafe did in the woods. He also knows his mother will die before he and Jewel return, but he wants Jewel to help him load the wagon.

Tull is sitting with Anse, who continues to complain about his troubles. Tull notices Vardaman, the youngest boy, bring a large fish into the yard. The boy struggles with the huge fish which seems "ashamed of being dead." Vardaman says he plans to show the fish to his mother. Tull knows that the work Cash is supposed to do for him will have to be postponed. However, he still hopes that Cash will work as carefully on his barn as he does on Addie's casket. Before the Tulls leave, Cora, Kate, and Eula discuss the possibility of Anse remarrying before cotton-picking time. The women say that Cash and Darl can now get married. When Eula mentions that Jewel can get married now, too, Kate responds that the girls in the neighborhood do not need to worry. She says that he will never get tied down.

Anse describes how his wife and his children have been a burden. He tells us how he has suffered for his family. He is toothless and cannot eat "God's own victuals," and claims he suffers because

his sons must work. Anse feels luck is against him though he has done no wrong. Vardaman reappears, covered in blood. He has cut up the large fish and asks if his mother is sick.

Darl seems to taunt Jewel by asking if he knows his mother is going to die. He also pushes Dewey Dell to admit that she wants Addie to die so they can go to Jefferson, where she might find a way out of her pregnancy.

Peabody remarks that Anse has called him because he finally wore Addie out. He wonders if it would be right to cure her just to make her continue living with Anse. Because the house is at the top of an incredibly steep hill, the old doctor must be hauled up by rope. Peabody can see that Addie is dying and asks Anse why he didn't call for him sooner. Dewey Dell calls them into the bedroom as Addie is just about to die. The dying woman forces Peabody from the room with her intense stare. As he goes to the porch, he hears her call Cash's name.

Though he is not present, Darl describes Addie's deathbed scene. She searches the room for Jewel and, missing him, calls out to Cash. As he holds up the boards to show her how the casket is progressing, Addie lies back and dies. Dewey Dell begins to wail, Vardaman runs from the room, and Anse exclaims, "God's will be done . . . Now I can get them teeth." Darl, working far off with Jewel, says to him, "She is dead, Jewel. Addie Bundren is dead."

Analysis

Faulkner combines two narrative techniques in *As I Lay Dying*: stream-of-consciousness and multiple narrators. Faulkner became known for using different narrators to tell a single story, each from his or her own perspective.

The stream-of-consciousness style permits narrators to speak their minds. Their thoughts appear unplanned and unmediated and, therefore, more true and immediate. We may or may not like a character or agree with him or her, but we can trust that the speaker truly believes in what he or she is saying.

Multiple narration shifts back and forth among the many characters providing the reader with differing viewpoints of the same events. It also complicates the search for the truth. Cora Tull's view of the relationship between Addie and Darl, and Addie and Jewel, is different from what we learn of their feelings for Addie in

their respective narratives. Faulkner is stressing that the truth—or history—of an event or situation is not contained in any one viewpoint. Anse views himself as a victim; Jewel and Peabody see Addie as the victim. The reader is forced to examine each narrative carefully in order to piece together the whole picture. Had the story been told only from Cora Tull's or Anse's point of view, it might turn out to be a very different story. It would have stressed their concerns. Cora is religious and concerned with that aspect of life. Anse is self-centered and believes everything bad happens to him.

Faulkner also uses figurative language in describing scenery and characters. He uses metaphors and similes to create more vivid images of the scenery and characters. For example, he refers to Addie's eyes as sputtering candles and, a few pages later, as oil lamps which are about to go out. These metaphors and similes remind the reader of the larger and more common metaphor of the "spark of life." However, rather than relying on well-known metaphors, he creates new ones. The new images are also closer to the rural, farm world which his characters inhabit. Her eyes are oil lamps or candles, not electric lights. Faulkner's figurative language adds to the tone of the novel and helps us envision the world of the Bundrens.

The language used by each character is very different and reveals even more than the subject he or she is discussing. A parallel can be made between the characters and their language because their words are an important extension of who and what they are.

Cora Tull uses many religious references. However, she speaks them the way a child does, in a repetitious, parrot-like fashion. She does not appear to fully understand her religion, just as she does not understand the relationships in the Bundren household. Jewel uses harsh or obscene language, highlighting his personality and the differences between him and his brother, Darl. Jewel's violent language parallels his quick temper and his brute and forceful actions. Jewel is his language—hostile and angry. Darl, unlike most of the others, is descriptive in his narrative and notices small details. He employs both metaphors and similes to create a vivid description of his brother, Jewel. He says, "His pales eyes [are] like wood set into his wooden face" giving him "the rigid gravity of a cigar store Indian dressed in patched overalls." In describing Jewel's

fancy, spotted horse, Darl says, "Then Jewel sees him, glinting for a gaudy instant among the blue shadows." Darl also gives creative and articulate descriptions of other characters and of the Bundren farm and its environment. His use of language is very different from that of his family members and neighbors. It is yet another characteristic which sets him apart from people, making them consider him "queer." The majority of the other characters speak plainly, using the everyday language suited to their time and place.

The description of the house and surrounding landscape should be examined carefully. The Bundren house is built on a nearly inaccessible hill. The house is built on a slant so that voices seem to speak out of thin air. The sun looks like a bloody egg, the air is sulphurous, and the path is like a crooked limb. As later sections will indicate, the use of dark, gothic images will set the tone for the journey.

In this first section we learn about family relationships and concerns. We discover that Jewel and Darl have a strained relationship, that Dewey Dell has come to view her mother's death as an opportunity to seek help, and that though neighbors realize that Anse uses people, they are compelled to continue to do his work for him. The major character conflicts established in this section are between Darl and Jewel, Addie and Anse, and Dewey Dell and Darl.

The most interesting narrator in this first section is Darl. He seems to have second sight, to be omniscient. He knows what happened between Dewey Dell and Lafe, and he knows his sister needs to get to Jefferson. He tells Jewel their mother is going to die, though Jewel thinks she will get better. Though he and Jewel are working some distance away at the time of Addie's death, he is able to narrate the deathbed scene and even gets inside his sister's mind as she follows Peabody onto the porch and considers asking him to help her. Finally, he is aware of the moment of Addie's death and informs Jewel that she is now dead.

The first section, up to Addie's death, establishes the characters and their relationships and prepares us for the main action of the story: the family's journey to Jefferson with Addie's corpse. It also requires the reader to examine what each character says and the language used to express his or her thoughts.

Study Questions

1. Why are Cora and Vernon Tull, Kate, and Eula at the Bundren house?

2. What reason does Anse give for not working?

3. How do we know Cora Tull is not a reliable narrator?

4. How does Dewey Dell explain why she got pregnant?

5. What reason does Tull give for people continuing to help Anse out?

6. Who is Anse's main concern?

7. Why is Peabody upset at being called to the Bundren's farm?

8. Why didn't Anse send for Peabody sooner?

9. What is the function of the italicized sections in Darl's narratives?

10. What are Anse's and Dewey Dell's actual motives for getting to Jefferson?

Answers

1. They are being neighborly by helping Anse Bundren and watching by Addie Bundren's deathbed.

2. Anse does not dare to work because, over 20 years ago, he became sick from working in the sun too long. He now believes that if he works, he might sweat and die.

3. Cora believes that Darl is Addie's favorite and that Jewel does not care for her. However, just before her narrative, we see that Darl and Anse were less concerned with being at Addie's deathbed than Jewel was.

4. Dewey Dell says she could not help it. Whether or not she went with Lafe into the shady grove depended upon whether or not her cotton sack was full. She blames fate, not herself.

5. Tull says that he, like everyone else, has been doing things for Anse for so long that it's become a habit.

6. Anse's main concern is his own bad luck, misfortunes, and

needs. He expresses little interest in the problems or needs of his family members.

7. Peabody is upset about going to the Bundrens' because there is a storm coming, and because the road to the house is so steep, he has to be hauled up by rope. He also wonders whether it is ethical to save Addie just to have her get more worn out by Anse.

8. Anse says he didn't send for Peabody sooner because he had other things to do: he was looking after the boys who were working and he was thinking.

9. The italicized sections in Darl's narratives indicate his ability to see/understand things without being there. It makes it seem as if he is in two places at one time: in one place physically, in another mentally.

10. Dewey Dell wants someone to find someone who can help her end her pregnancy; Anse wants to get a set of teeth for himself.

Suggested Essay Topics

1. Describe the setting by examining the words and phrases used to depict the Bundrens' home and the surrounding elements (weather, sky, etc).

2. Select a character (Jewel, Darl, or Anse) and compare and contrast the ways in which he is described by other narrators who talk about him.

3. Examine the ways in which each of the characters in this first section view Addie Bundren on her deathbed and discuss their emotional responses to her death (for example, sympathetic, caring, worried, etc.).

4. In the first part of the novel, we learn that Anse Bundren's wife is on her deathbed. By making a close study of what Anse talks about and says how does he feel about his wife's impending death? What does Anse's main concern seem to be?

Unit 2

New Characters:

Armstid: *neighbor to the Bundrens; attends Addie's funeral*

Reverend Whitfield: *preacher who conducts Addie's funeral*

Uncle Billy Varner: *older neighbor; attends Addie's funeral*

Jody: *Uncle Billy's son*

Quick: *neighbor to the Bundrens; attends Addie's funeral*

Houston: *neighbor to the Bundrens; attends Addie's funeral*

Littlejohn: *neighbor to the Bundrens; attends Addie's funeral*

Summary

Upset by his mother's death, Vardaman rushes from the house and to the barn where he takes out his frustration by beating the horses. Dewey Dell, preoccupied with her problem, agonizes over Peabody's ability to help her if she could only tell him. She finds Vardaman hiding in the barn and sends him in to supper. She feels lonely and remains in the barn, talking to the cow that she is milking.

In order to persuade her brother to go along on the trip to Jefferson, Dewey Dell promises Vardaman that they will get bananas to eat and a shiny toy for him when they get to the city. Vardaman runs away to the Tulls' house. They bring him back home and remark how Vardaman kept opening the window in Addie's room so she could breathe and how he bored airholes in the coffin for Addie. Some of those holes bored into her face.

The family is up all night finishing the coffin, working through rain and darkness, in order to have it ready by morning. Cash insists on making the job perfect.

In the morning, the news comes that the bridge is washed out. Jewel and Darl, hampered by the washed-out bridge, arrive home three days after their mother has died. Addie's death seems to have changed Anse. He now stands taller and is self-important. Neighbors gather for the funeral service, and buzzards circle above the house, scenting the decaying corpse.

Jewel, Cash, and Darl help carry the coffin out of the house and down the steep path. Darl taunts Jewel, who loses control of his emotions and, in doing so, loses control of the coffin as well. Addie and her casket go careening down the side of the hill. The family loads the coffin on the wagon and prepares to leave. A clean-shaven Anse complains that his family is too concerned with their own needs and is not showing proper respect for the dead. Cash is concerned with carrying his tools with him, and Dewey Dell says she must carry cakes to town for Mrs. Tull. Vardaman is interested in getting his toy train. Anse seems especially annoyed that Jewel rides his high-spirited, spotted horse rather than ride in the wagon. He also criticizes Darl for laughing while sitting in the wagon with his mother's coffin. Anse again bemoans his hard life and feels that the false teeth he will get in Jefferson will be a comfort to him.

Analysis

There is a tradition of dark, gothic horror in Southern literature. Faulkner employs these gothic horror elements throughout the story. Though the novel is a tragedy, he also injects some "black comedy" or dark humor into the story. The macabre scenes lend a horror-film feeling to the novel. For example, descriptions of the Bundren house, off-center and built on an inaccessible hill, make it seem like a haunted house. When Addie dies, a storm rages. The air is described as sulphurous, a word used in descriptions of Hell. The favorite phrases used by Jewel, Addie's favorite son, are Goddamn, damn, and hell. Darl has the ability to know what is happening somewhere else. Faulkner italicizes those parts of Darl's narrative which are not straight narration in order to draw attention to Darl's peculiar ability to "read" people or to presage things which are happening somewhere else. Adding to the macabre atmosphere is Addie Bundren's insistence on being buried in her own home ground in Jefferson. Her body begins to decompose and smell while

the family awaits Darl's and Jewel's return before they transport her casket.

The association between animals and people becomes more evident in this section of the novel. Anse is described as buzzard-like. Vardaman confuses his mother and the fish he caught and cut up for dinner. He says to the horses, "You kilt my maw!" as he strikes at them with a stick. Darl tells Jewel, who has already been described as being one with his horse, that his mother is a horse. Dewey Dell, unhappy with her pregnancy, identifies with the moaning cows which she milks. She feels as burdened and as helpless as they are. She says, "I feel like a wet seed wild in the hot blind earth." The words and phrases used to describe her feelings and appearance make her almost indistinguishable from the cows and from nature. Finally, the buzzards begin to circle around Addie's unembalmed corpse and to follow her as the coffin travels to Jefferson. The distinction between people and animals is blurred. Anse's posture is similar to that of a buzzard. The metaphor can be extended to Anse's character: like a buzzard, he seems to feed off Addie's death. As her body rots, he appears neater, cleaner, and more alert than when we first met him.

In addition to drawing parallels between his characters and animals, Faulkner borrows some ideas from witchcraft, devil worship, and vampirism to add to the gothic flavor of the novel. Addie is placed in her coffin upside down, an inversion of traditional burial which calls to mind the inverted crosses used as symbols in witchcraft or devil worship. In folklore on witches, animals are important as "familiars." A witch is often depicted with a cat, bat, or some other animal. In folklore, a witch or devil often takes the shape of an animal. Vardaman's boring of auger holes into the coffin to permit his mother to breathe recalls tales of vampires who only rest in their coffins. Vampires also need to rest in the soil of their own land. Addie wants to be buried in the soil of her family plot in Jefferson. Adding to this interpretation is how Addie seems to be alive in her casket. Darl remarks that it is as if her body is moving inside the coffin as they carry it. The casket breaks free of their hands and coasts down the hill as if it cannot get away from the Bundren house fast enough. Some folk beliefs include the idea that evil spirits cannot cross a bridge or body of water. The washing out of the bridge, preventing Addie's body from crossing it, reinforces the notion of Addie as an evil spirit.

Each narrator becomes a much more fully developed character in this section. It is clear that for Anse, Dewey Dell, Vardaman, and Cash, Addie's death represents an opportunity for satisfying a personal desire, whether it is buying a set of teeth, getting an abortion, finding a toy, or being preoccupied with tools and craftsmanship. Most of Addie's family members do not seem moved by her death.

Cash's sole preoccupation is the casket and how well it has been made. He is concerned with beveling the edges of the casket. He also is obsessive in his insistence that the casket be properly balanced on the wagon. One of Cash's chapters is a simple list of the 13 reasons for building the casket as he has. Dewey Dell does not mourn her mother. She mourns her own lamentable condition of being pregnant and alone. Vardaman, behaving as any child might, looks at the trip as an adventure which offers a shiny toy and exotic fruit at its end. Jewel and Darl are the only ones preoccupied with Addie. Jewel is intent on getting his mother's body to Jefferson with dignity and fulfilling her wish. Darl challenges Jewel's obsession by taunting his brother about Addie's death. He laughs at the absurdity of making the 40-mile trip to Jefferson with an already decaying corpse. Anse calls his laughter disrespect for Addie and remarks that it is Darl's habit of unprovoked laughter which makes folk consider him odd. Darl's narratives are the most philosophical, complicated, and confusing sections of the novel. In one passage, in which he describes sleep as "is-not," it becomes clear that Darl is a thoughtful character whose ideas and concerns are far different from those around him. It is as if he is trying to discover who he is and where his place is in the world. He says, "How often have I lain beneath rain on a strange roof, thinking of home." Darl appears to feel that he is not at home where he is. Indeed, his family members and his neighbors comment on his strangeness as a sort of foreignness. He is like a traveller in another country, trying to make sense out of the words and actions of those he encounters.

A definite tension exists between the grim, violent, and silent Jewel and the omniscient, thoughtful, and peculiar Darl. The tension grows as the journey progresses, and its focal point seems to be Addie's wish to be buried in Jefferson.

Study Questions

1. How does Peabody's team of horses get chased away from the Bundren farm?

2. How did Lafe respond when Dewey Dell told him she was pregnant?

3. How do Cora and Vernon Tull discover that Addie has died?

4. Before boring the holes in the coffin, how else does Vardaman attempt to provide his dead mother with air?

5. Why does Armstid suggest Anse bury Addie in New Hope?

6. Why does Cash walk with a limp?

7. According to Cora, what reward has Addie finally received?

8. Why does Cash take his tools with him on the trip to Jefferson?

9. What other indication does Darl give that he knows Dewey Dell is pregnant?

10. Why does Anse claim to be "the chosen of the Lord"?

Answers

1. Vardaman has struck at the horses in retaliation and chases them away, because he feels Peabody is somehow to blame for his mother's death.

2. Lafe told her that he was more worried than she was. He gave her money to buy some medicine which would cause an abortion.

3. Peabody's team appears, followed by Vardaman. The boy is soaking wet and incoherent, and the Tulls realize that Addie must have died.

4. Vardaman sneaks into his mother's room and keeps opening up the windows by her deathbed.

5. The storm is going to wash out the bridge to Jefferson, and the family would not get through without taking more time and effort.

6. Cash broke his leg when he fell more than 28 feet from a church roof on which he had been working.

7. Cora says of Addie, "Wherever she went [when she died], she has her reward in being free of Anse Bundren."

8. He plans to stop off at the Tulls' home on the return trip in order to repair the Tull's roof.

9. When Dewey Dell steps into the wagon to go to Jefferson, Darl notes that her dress is beginning to get tight.

10. Anse, who believes that he suffers more misfortunes than anyone, also believes that the Lord chastises those that He loves.

Suggested Essay Topics

1. Examine the narratives which connect any one of the following pairs and discuss how the narrators—and Faulkner —use animal imagery: Jewel and his horse; Dewey Dell and the cows; Addie and the fish; Anse and a steer.

2. Anse claims that he is being chastised by God. Describe the physical and personality changes he undergoes after Addie's death. Discuss whether his life now seems to be better, worse, or the same as it was.

3. Describe Vardaman Bundren's reaction to his mother's death and the way his response is treated by others. As a grieving child, what does Vardaman seem to be lacking?

4. Faulkner makes the relationship between some characters clear fairly early in the novel. For example, it is easy to see the tension between Darl and Jewel. Examine Cash's narratives, what he says, and what others say about him. What kind of person does cash seem to be? What are his main concerns? How does it seem that the other characters view him?

SECTION FOUR

Unit 3

New Characters:

Samson: *distant neighbor to the Bundrens who lets them stay overnight at his barn when they are on their way to Jefferson*

MacCallum: *distant neighbor to the Bundrens*

Rachel: *Samson's wife*

Flem Snopes: *man who brought a number of wild horses to town; Jewel's horse is related to a Snopes' horse*

Summary

Some neighbors and townspeople, watching the Bundren wagon pass, believe that Addie has been buried already and that the Bundrens are just traveling. In attempting to notify them that the bridge is washed out, Quick notices the stench from the wagon and realizes it's Addie's corpse. When Quick and Samson both try to convince Anse to bury Addie in nearby New Hope, Dewey Dell becomes frightened that she will not be able to find the doctor or medicine she needs for an abortion. She convinces her father to stick to Addie's request to be buried in Jefferson. The Bundrens decline Samson's offer to let them sleep in the house and try to decline eating with their hosts. Samson's wife, Rachel, is outraged that Anse has been toting Addie's corpse around for four days. In the morning, after the Bundrens have left the barn, Samson says that he can still smell and sense that death has been there. As he turns to leave, he thinks he sees someone who has been left behind. However, it is a buzzard which slowly exits the barn while watching Samson over his shoulder.

Dewey Dell is afraid that Darl will convince Anse to bury Addie at New Hope. She fantasizes about killing him. Darl taunts both Dewey Dell and Jewel about his ability to convince Anse to stop in New Hope.

Tull finds the family at the river crossing. The bridge is half under water, and Anse sits in his wagon, staring at the situation as if he welcomes hardship. Dewey Dell is vexed. Tull asks Darl's opinion about attempting to cross the river. He says that Darl looks at people as if he is inside of them and knows everything they are doing. Tull thinks this is why people consider Darl peculiar. When Tull suggests they wait another day to see if the river falls, Jewel tells him to go to hell. He is determined to cross the river. Vardaman, Dewey Dell, and Anse will walk across the bridge, and Tull and the three older boys will lead the wagon across. Tull refuses to use his mule to help cross.

Darl recalls when Jewel was fifteen. He says his brother was getting thinner and falling asleep while working. Addie worried about him, but Anse insisted that he had to help out with the work. Addie prepared extra food for him and sat up by his bed, worrying over him. Cash and Darl thought he was having an affair with some girl or married woman because Jewel began to stay out all night. Dewey Dell does Jewel's milking and other chores. Five months later, they discovered that Jewel was working an extra job in order to buy a fancy, spotted horse from Quick. Anse was angry at Jewel and acted as if the horse cost the family money. Cash supported Jewel and said it cost them nothing. An angry Jewel told Anse that he would kill the horse rather than feed it from Anse's store of grain. That night, Addie cried by Jewel's bed as he slept, and Darl indicates that it was then he knew something about Addie's relationship to Jewel.

Tull helps Vardaman, Anse, and Dewey Dell across the bridge. He warns them that it would be better to wait another day before crossing; the river might fall enough to make crossing easier. Anse just repeats that he gave Addie his word that he would take her to Jefferson. He will not be swayed. Tull is angry and cannot understand why one more day would matter. He thinks they are more concerned with getting to Jefferson to eat a sack of bananas.

Darl and Cash are on the wagon when they cross the river, while Jewel crosses on his horse. The oaks which used to mark the fording place in the river have been cut down. Jewel goes ahead, on horseback, to feel out the shallowest part for crossing. Vernon Tull, on the bank, waves them farther downstream. They find the ford, but Cash warns them that the coffin is not properly balanced in the wagon. As they attempt to cross, a log rises up and disengages the rope Cash and Jewel were using to lead the wagon across. It overturns the mules and hits the wagon, causing it to rise perpendicular to the current. One mule is hit and dragged under water. Cash tells Darl to jump clear and head for shore. The wagon turns again, and the last thing Darl sees are the mules turning over in the water.

The coffin floats free of the wagon, and those on the bank shout to Darl to catch it. Vardaman believes Darl can get it because he is a good "grabbler." However, he is surprised to see Darl come up empty-handed from the river.

Cora Tull tells her husband that it was "the hand of God" which overturned the Bundren's wagon, not a log. Tull describes how Jewel and his horse, Cash and his toolbox, and Addie all went spilling into the river. He is angry at Anse and holds him responsible for putting everyone at risk. Cash, who cannot swim, hangs on to the side of Jewel's horse and is kicked by the animal and injured. As they pull him out of the water, they can see where the rope is taut, still connected to the wagon under water. A dead and bloated pig floats by them.

Cash is sick from his injury. The others, including Tull, go diving into the river to retrieve his tools. Anse looks on, bemoaning his own misfortune. Anse says it is lucky that Cash has broken the same leg which had been broken from his fall, long ago. Cash says he told them the coffin was not balanced properly.

Analysis

It becomes more apparent that Anse seems to enjoy all the misfortunes which befall the family while on this trip. He treats each setback or accident as if it were a personal test of his faith or will. Nonetheless, of all the characters, he is the one who does the least amount of work or actual suffering.

It is nearly five days since Addie died. Adding to the indignity of her decomposing body are: the holes in her face; being placed reverse in the coffin; being jumbled up inside from coasting downhill and falling into the river; and being drenched from her

fall into the river. She is becoming ghoulish, in a sense. She now has an escort of buzzards following the family on its progress, and the smell of rotting flesh seems to affect everyone except for the Bundrens themselves.

Darl seems determined to prevent Addie from reaching Jefferson. He taunts Jewel and threatens Dewey Dell by making her realize that he can get Anse to bury Addie in New Hope if he suggests it. Darl realizes that Anse's "sacred" promise to his wife is kept only because it means he will get a new set of teeth. Darl is able to see everyone for what they are. As others have suggested, he is considered peculiar by most folk because of this ability.

It is important, again, to note the language that the characters use. Anse repeats the same phrase or ideas—concerning his misfortunes—over and over. Though he may vary his words somewhat, he never actually says anything else. Anse's words are empty of meaning. Whereas Cora Tull may believe that she understands what her religious phrases mean, Anse is content to speak without imparting any meaning to his words. When the family arrives at the washed-out bridge, Tull notes that Anse sits in the wagon saying, "I give her my promised word in the presence of the Lord, I reckon it ain't no need to worry." However, Tull also notes that Anse does not start the mules. Typically, he waits for others to move to action.

As in an earlier chapter, in which Cash described the steps involved in designing his casket, Faulkner again demonstrates Cash's single-mindedness by devoting an entire chapter to the casket. After it has toppled off the wagon and into the river, Cash's chapter reads, "It wasn't on a balance. I told them that if they wanted it to tote and ride on a balance, they would have to" This chapter is only one and a half sentences long. Faulkner cuts it off in mid-sentence to indicate that Cash has passed out because of his accident. It also shows how, in spite of his accident and the turmoil which everyone had just gone through, Cash remains preoccupied with his handiwork and generally oblivious to the other characters.

The background information on how Jewel purchased his horse, which Darl presents, provides insight on the unusual relationship between Addie and her husband and children. Though Cora had earlier claimed that Darl and his mother shared a special bond, it is clear that Addie has favored Jewel above her other children. She had them cover for him when he was unable to perform his chores, and she has sat by his bed, cooked especially for him, and cried for him. In following these narratives, it is easy to see how people's perceptions might be incorrect, colored by their own beliefs, or presented according to their own interests. For example, Cash is most concerned with his handiwork. He views Addie's death in terms of carpentry. Cora's perceptions are based, in large part, on her religion and beliefs. She assumes that others must view things the same way. Faulkner wants readers to read carefully and to examine the motives and bases for people's ideas and thoughts.

Darl's relationship with Jewel is clearly colored by each boy's relationship with his mother. Darl does not seem to consider Addie his mother, at least not in the usual sense. He is intent on examining the relationships between family members. Darl says that there is some deceitfulness associated with Addie. He is able to see past the superficial and have insight into her character. He is the only one who can look beyond a person's words or actions and know something about the people around him.

Vardaman's mother finally does "become a fish" as her coffin floats in the river. The little boy is surprised, however, that Darl has not been able to rescue Addie's coffin. It is obvious that Darl is as intent to prevent Addie from reaching Jefferson as Jewel is that she get there. The struggle over Addie's body becomes a metaphor for the struggle over her soul. The struggle between Darl and Jewel can be interpreted as the fight between good and evil. However, it is not entirely clear who is right or wrong or how right or wrong either one might be. Again, Faulkner requires the reader to examine each narrative juxtaposed against one another before arriving at any conclusion.

Study Questions

1. Why won't the Bundrens accept food or decent shelter from Samson?

2. What does Samson consider to be the way to show respect to Addie?

3. What does the buzzard in the barn remind Samson of?

4. Who decides that they will cross the river?

5. Why didn't they get a doctor for Jewel when they thought he was sick years ago?

6. Why did Cash hope that Jewel was *not* having an affair with a married woman?

7. Who followed Jewel to find out where he was spending all of his time?

8. Why was Tull so intent on getting Cash out of the river?

9. What happens to the Bundren's team of mules?

10. How does Darl describe the coldness of the river?

Answers

1. Anse repeats that they do not want to be "beholden" to anyone. Nonetheless, though he declines hospitality, he manages to get favors from people because he whines, complains, and wears a "hang dog" look which elicits their sympathy.

2. He says the best way to show respect to a woman who has been dead four days is to get her buried as soon as possible.

3. He says the buzzard looks just like a "spraddle-legged" and "old bald-headed" man as it exits the barn, looking back over its shoulder.

4. Cash and Jewel make the decision to go forward and cross the river.

5. Anse didn't want to spend the money and said it was not necessary.

6. Cash felt that a young fellow should not waste his youth on someone or something which was safe; but, he should save it for something newer, better, and brighter.

7. Cash followed Jewel and discovered that he had been working nights, clearing a field for Quick.

8. Cash did not know how to swim.

9. The mules, caught in the harness and reins, are tied to the wagon and drown in the river.

10. He says it feels "like hands molding and prodding at the very bones."

Suggested Essay Topics

1. Compare and contrast Cora Tull's language with that of Jewel and discuss how it serves to develop each character.

2. Examine Dewey Dell's narrative. What does it tell us about her relationship with her mother, with Darl, and with God? Discuss whether or not she believes in God.

3. Study Darl's narrative which describes how Jewel got his horse. Describe what his narrative tells us about the relationship of the parents and children in the Bundren household.

4. The washed out bridge is the first real obstacle which the Bundrens encounter on the journey to Jefferson. Each one reacts differently to the problem. Discuss their reactions and how each reaction is appropriate to that character. How is the outcome of the crossing typical of Jewel's actions in general?

SECTION FIVE

Unit 4

New Characters:

Lula: *Armstid's wife*

Snopes: *a horsetrader; nephew to Flem; sold new mules to the Bundrens after theirs drown*

Eustace Grimm: *a man who works for Snopes*

Moseley: *pharmacist in the town of Mottson*

Albert: *Moseley's assistant*

The Marshal: *nameless marshal for the town of Mottson*

Suratt: *a man who had a talking machine to sell*

Grummet: *owner of the hardware store in Mottson*

Summary

   Cora relates discussions she had with Addie about sin and salvation. Cora says Addie was never really religious, not even after Brother Whitfield tried so hard to save her soul. Though Addie insists that she has sinned and suffered for it, Cora tells her that she cannot know what sin is. Cora believes Addie's biggest sin was in preferring Jewel (whom she says never loved her) over Darl (who was touched by God and did love her). When Cora asks her what her salvation will be, Addie responds "He will save me from the water and from the fire. Even though I have laid down my life, he will save me." Cora realizes Addie does not mean God, but Jewel. She prays for Addie's soul because she says she has committed sacrilege.

   Addie's narrative informs us that she used to be a schoolteacher.

She despised the schoolchildren and looked forward to whipping them so they would be aware of her. She says her father taught her that the reason for living was to prepare to stay dead for a long time.

She says she "took Anse." She noticed him loitering around the school where she taught, trying to get up the nerve to speak to her. He proposed to her and said he had no relatives. She said she had relatives in Jefferson but that they were all dead. She has never had any other kind.

After they married and she gave birth to Cash, she felt violated and alone. She was angry with Anse and herself for getting pregnant with Darl and made Anse promise to take her back to Jefferson when she died. Addie is preoccupied with the meaninglessness of words. She is disappointed in her marriage, because she does not communicate with Anse. She says that he is dead to her. She has an affair with the preacher, whom she meets in the woods. However, when it is over, she does not miss him. While having the affair, she does not give herself to Anse. When the affair has been over two months, she realizes that she is pregnant with the preacher's child, Jewel. She says she gave Anse Dewey Dell as a way of negating Jewel. She gave him Vardaman to make up for the child which should have been his. She says that now that Anse has three children which are his, not hers, she can prepare to die. She criticizes people like Cora Tull and says that prayer and salvation are just words to them. They do not understand what the words mean.

Whitfield, in his narrative, reveals that he confessed his sin (adultery) to God on discovering that Addie was dying. He says that God commanded him to correct the sin by asking Anse to forgive him. He journeys to the Bundren house considering how he will confess to Anse and ask his forgiveness. He wants to confess to Anse, because he is afraid Addie might make the confession first, on her deathbed. Whitfield considers the floods and dangers he encounters on the way there to be a test of his intention. Because he forges ahead in the storm, he believes he is in earnest. When Tull's youngest girl informs him that Addie is already dead, Whitfield praises God and says that her death is proof that God accepted the will for the deed. He no longer believes it is incumbent upon him to confess, especially since Addie did not tell anyone. He enters the house and gives it God's blessing.

Darl tells us that, in addition to injuring his leg again, Cash also might have been kicked in the stomach by the horse. Armstid offers to put the family up overnight. The soaking of the coffin helped take away some of the stench which had been making people avoid them. Cash is taken into the house to be looked after by the women. Uncle Billy tries to set Cash's leg until they can get to a doctor.

Anse talks with Armstid about getting another team of mules. Armstid says he is being picky and should think about buying mules from Snopes. Anse has a few drinks of whiskey with Armstid and becomes talkative. Later on, Jewel and Anse plan to strike a deal with Snopes for some mules. Jewel stays behind and lets Anse ride the horse, but he is worried about the animal. The sun has dried the coffin, and the smell becomes unbearable. Armstid sees Vardaman chasing 12 buzzards off the coffin. Jewel, angered by Armstid's implication that the coffin stinks, insists on moving it. Darl prefers to wait until Anse returns so they can leave. Because Anse is taking so long to strike a deal, and because he has no money or property to trade with, Armstid thinks he may have to offer his own mules to the Bundrens, just to get them to leave. Anse returns, looking both pleased with himself and "hang-dog." He says he got a team by mortgaging some of his farm implements. However, the family knows they aren't worth enough for a team. Darl realizes that Anse has stolen eight dollars from Cash's pocket which Cash had been saving to buy a record player. When the sum is still short, Anse admits to having traded Jewel's horse. When Jewel bristles at his news, Anse replies that he's been saving 15 years to buy some teeth. Jewel jumps on his horse and tears off down the road. Armstid thinks he ran away, but they learn he brought the horse to Snopes to seal the trade.

Cash's leg is in very bad shape. Nevertheless, he insists that they go on. Jewel has not returned to join the family. They hitch up the Snopes' mules to Armstid's borrowed wagon and drive on. The buzzards continue to follow.

Dewey Dell visits Moseley's pharmacy in Mottson. She does not really know what to ask for. Moseley thinks she may be younger than she looks and is suffering menstrual problems for the first time. He thinks she is simply too shy to ask for help. When he finally discovers what she wants from him, he is outraged. He advises her to get her father to get Lafe to marry her. When she tells him that

Lafe said ten dollars would be enough to buy the abortion medicine, Moseley becomes angry and says that no one ever said that *his drugstore* would sell it. After she leaves, Moseley's assistant, Albert, tells the druggist about the scene the rest of the family made in town that afternoon. He said they stopped to buy cement to fix Cash's leg. However, the smell from the wagon was so bad that the townsfolk called the marshal. He ordered them to leave before they were charged with violating the public health law. He advises them to get proper care for Cash's leg. The people are relieved when the wagon finally pulls out of Mottson.

The Bundrens stop to make a cement cast for Cash's leg. Darl taunts Dewey Dell by mentioning that she must have had more trouble than she expected selling her cakes in Mottson. As they adjust the ropes, splints, and cement on Cash's leg, they see Jewel come walking up the road. He gets into the wagon, silent.

Vardaman seems glad Jewel has returned. The wagon continues on. Vardaman asks Darl where the buzzards go at night. He plans to stay up that night to watch where they go when the family is in the barn.

Darl asks Jewel, " . . . whose son are you?" He taunts him about his parents, saying his mother was a horse, but he does not know who his father was. Cash appears feverish. Below the cement cast, his leg and foot are turning bright red. Cash says it feels very hot, so they pour water over the cast to cool his leg. Darl and Vardaman go out to the apple tree where they have put Addie's coffin for the night. There is a cat lying on the coffin. Darl brings Vardaman to hear Addie talking inside the box, to hear her "little trickling bursts of secret and murmurous bubbling."

Analysis

This section gives some background on the relationships in the Bundren family. It is the only chance we get to hear Addie speak and it is interesting that her narrative appears after she has been dead. Its appearance later in the novel reinforces the image of Addie being alive in her coffin, the image of being one of the "living dead." Addie's narrative, being sandwiched between the narratives of two "religious" characters, also is significant. From her previous narratives and lines of dialogue, we know that Cora Tull is an unreliable narrator. Her long narrative here proves her to be a shallow and uncomprehending person who merely parrots the religious sentiments she has learned. Cora has no understanding, profound or otherwise, of the words she uses. Whitfield is an even better example. As a preacher, he should definitely practice what he preaches. Whitfield, however, conducts an adulterous affair with a married member of his church, does not recognize their child, and fails to confess and ask forgiveness for his sin. He is both a hypocrite and a coward.

Addie, like her favorite son, seems to be a violent person. She whips her schoolchildren in the same way Jewel whips his horse. It is their way of getting recognition, of making a physical connection with another being. Clearly, Addie and Jewel need the connection to be physical because they both realize that language will not work. Jewel's language is limited to curses. In beating his horse, he is cruel and loving at the same time. He is trying to get recognition from the animal by using physical feelings instead of words. Addie understands, from her experience with Cora, Whitfield, Anse, and others, that words are not the same as deeds or acts. She says that words "go straight up in a thin line, quick and harmless," but "doing goes long the earth, clinging to it." In figurative language, Faulkner has Addie express the inability of words to communicate. She says, " . . . We had had to use one another by words like spiders dangling by their mouths from a beam, swinging and twisting and never touching, and that only through the blows of the switch could my blood and their blood flow as one stream." The torturous image of a desperate spider struggling for connection describes Addie's feeling about language and about relationships. The spider is both vulnerable and horrible, hanging by his thread. Denied that connection, Addie must make others aware of her through the violence of the switch, through a physical joining. Her sinful union with Whitfield is another attempt at communication. However, she sees that has failed her, too.

What is most interesting is that Addie's narrative, like Darl's, is thoughtful and philosophical. She has been a teacher, someone whose business is communicating meanings to others. In her narrative, Addie says that even though she is married to Anse, and a mother many times, she is alone. She echoes Darl who also feels out of place, as if he does not have a home.

Addie says that she gave Anse three children, although there are four born to her and Anse. She may not be counting Dewey Dell, whom she said was born to "negative" the illegitimate Jewel. She might also be referring to Darl, whose birth angered her. She says, "Then I found that I had Darl. At first I would not believe it. Then I believed I would kill Anse. It was as though he had tricked me . . .." Addie's narrative makes clear that her connection with her children is peculiar. She does not share the typical attributes of motherhood which other characters want to apply to her.

By stealing Cash's money and Jewel's horse, Anse avoids using the money he has brought to buy teeth. He claims, as usual, that he suffers most, but as Addie would point out, the words and the actual physical reality do not correspond. When Cash appears worried about having his leg encased in cement, Anse is the one who coerces him into letting them "fix" it. His concern is not so much that Cash is injured, rather, he keeps repeating "we done bought it," making Cash feel as if his refusing would make him an ingrate. Though Anse says it will be easier on Cash, the fact is that it will be easier on Anse by saving the time and money which he would otherwise have to "waste" by bringing his son to a doctor.

Darl provokes Dewey Dell. Speaking in double entendres, phrases that can be taken two ways, he remarks: "Those cakes will be in fine shape by the time we get to Jefferson." The implication is that her pregnancy will have advanced. He also knows that she has not secured the medicine from Mottson's druggist and says, "You had more trouble than you expected, selling those cakes in Mottson." "Cakes" becomes a metaphor for Dewey Dell's pregnancy. He repeatedly asks Jewel, "Whose son are you?" It is as if Darl knows about Whitfield and Addie, and he also knows the words which will have the strongest effect on Jewel. Darl uses language in a way that touches others physically. Whereas Anse, Cora, and Cash speak words, Darl speaks meanings.

Study Questions

1. What does Cora believe was the relationship between Addie and Reverend Whitfield?

2. Where does Addie go when school lets out?

3. How does Addie feel about her father?

4. Are we sure Addie's kin are dead?

5. Who does Whitfield credit for Addie's not confessing about their affair?

6. What kind of doctoring does Uncle Billy usually practice?

7. Why doesn't Vardaman come in to dinner at Armstid's house?

8. What does Moseley suggest Dewey Dell use the ten dollars for?

9. How many days has Addie been dead by the time the family arrives in Mottson?

10. What is Cash's reaction to Anse's suggestion that they cover his broken leg with a cement cast?

Answers

1. Cora believes that Whitfield wanted to wrestle with Addie's spirit and fight the "vanity in her mortal heart" in order to save her soul.

2. Addie heads down the hill to the spring where it smells of damp, rotting leaves and fresh dirt.

3. She hates her father for having "planted" her.

4. Addie tells Anse that they are in the cemetery, and we assume that she means they are dead.

5. Whitfield says that God, in his infinite wisdom, restrained her from telling her family about her sin.

6. Uncle Billy usually takes care of horses or mules.

7. He stays out in the yard chasing the buzzards away from Addie's casket.

8. Moseley says that he would never sell such medicine. He tells her to find Lafe and use the ten dollars to buy a wedding license.

9. Someone in Mottson says that Addie has been dead for eight days.

10. Cash seems to want to wait until they get to Jefferson, where a doctor could look at it. However, Anse reminds him that they already spent the money on the cement and pressures Cash into letting them do it.

Suggested Essay Topics

1. By examining the three portraits of Whitfield from this section—Cora's, Addie's, and Whitfield's own self-portrait—and relying on the information presented, create a composite description of what you think Whitfield is actually like.

2. How does the exchange between Moseley and Dewey Dell demonstrate Addie's contention that words themselves are meaningless and do not permit people to connect?

3. The section of the novel permits us a closer look at the relationship between Jewel and his horse. Through a close examination of Jewel's actions and words, the words and actions of Darl concerning Jewel and his horse, and the observations of others, draw a parallel between the reaction Jewel has to the loss of his mother and the loss of his horse.

4. Anse is constantly reminding people that he will not "Be beholden" to anyone. What exactly does he mean by this? Examine the family's stay at Armstid's and discuss what, if anything, Anse takes or refuses from others. Considering the needs of his famiily members, is he being selfless or selfish?

Unit 5

New Characters:

Gillespie: *farmer who lets the Bundrens stay over at his place*

Mack: *Gillespie's son*

Three negroes: *these people who are passed by the Bundren wagon*

A white man: *person passed by the Bundren wagon; he nearly fights with Jewel*

Two officials: *lawmen who come to take Darl to the asylum in Jackson because of his burning down Gillespie's barn*

Skeet MacGowan: *drugstore clerk in Jefferson*

Jody: *MacGowan's friend; another drugstore clerk*

Alford: *doctor or lawyer mentioned by MacGowan; suggested as someone to whom Dewey Dell might go for help*

"The old man": *Jefferson druggist and Skeet's and Jody's boss*

Mrs. Bundren: *a new wife Anse Bundren finds in Jefferson*

Summary

Darl brings Vardaman out to the apple tree under which Addie's coffin rests. Darl tells the boy that Addie is talking to God and that she wants Him to hide her from the sight of man so she can "lay down her life." They hear Addie turn in her coffin. Vardaman keeps repeating that he saw something which Dewey Dell told him not to tell anyone else about. Vardaman and Dewey Dell sleep on the Gillespie porch. The boy is waiting to discover where the buzzards go at night. Darl, Jewel, Gillespie, and his son carry Addie into the barn at night. After they leave, Vardaman goes down by the barn to find the buzzards.

The barn is on fire. The coffin can be seen through the open door of the barn. Jewel, Gillespie, Mack, Anse, Vardaman, and Dewey Dell rush from the house to the fire. Darl is already there. The men pass the coffin and rush to get the cows, mules, and horses out of the barn. Frightened by the flames, the animals must have their heads wrapped in the men's nightshirts before they will dare to pass through the flames. Once the animals are out, Jewel rushes to go back and rescue Addie's coffin. Darl tries to stop him, but he is determined to save his mother. Jewel upends the coffin and tumbles it, one end over the other until, covered with flaming embers and smelling of scorched flesh, he and the coffin crash through the barn's doorway to safety.

They bring Addie's body back under the apple tree. Cash's leg is turning black. They have to crack the cast off with a flat iron and a hammer. Gillespie berates them for being so foolish and encasing the leg in concrete. In removing it, Cash loses skin, and the leg bleeds. Jewel's back has been badly burned, and Dewey Dell puts some medicine on it. Darl is out by the apple tree, lying on his mother's coffin and crying. Vardaman tells him he need not cry since Jewel got her out of the fire.

Just outside of Jefferson, Dewey Dell asks Anse to stop the wagon so she can go into the bushes. She takes with her the newspaper wrapped package which is supposed to be Cora Tull's cakes. When she comes out, she is wearing her Sunday best. On the outskirts of Jefferson they pass rows of negro cabins. The wagon passes three black men on the road who recoil in horror and disgust when met with the stench from the wagon. Jewel, angered by their exclamation, curses at them. A white man, ahead of them on the road, thinks Jewel has cursed at him. Darl tries to restrain Jewel, and he notices the man has an open knife in his hand. Darl tells the man Jewel is not himself and gets Jewel to apologize. The wagon drives into Jefferson with Jewel, like a guardian gargoyle, riding the hub of the wheel. As they ride to the town square, citizens are aghast at both the sight and the smell.

It is revealed that Darl set Gillespie's barn on fire in order to burn Addie's body. In order to avoid being sued by Gillespie, they plan to have Darl taken away to an insane asylum in Jackson. Jewel

suggests that they tie him up so that he will not burn the wagon or the horses. Cash wonders whether Darl is entirely crazy and thinks that it might have been better had Jewel not retrieved Addie's body from the river. He thinks burning the body might have been a clean way to get it off their hands. Nonetheless, he thinks Darl should not have burned someone's barn.

Darl wants to bring Cash to the doctor's immediately. Though Anse wants to bury Addie first, he says they have no spade to dig with. When Anse says it will cost money to buy one, Darl asks, "Do you begrudge her it?" Anse wants to borrow a spade and randomly suggests a house at which to stop and ask for one. The sound of a gramophone is coming from the house. Cash feels that Anse has selected this house on purpose. When Darl suggests that he or Jewel could go to the door, Anse says he will go himself. He is in the house a long time, and as he leaves, he waves to a woman at the window.

When they leave the cemetery after Addie's burial, the men from Jackson jump onto the wagon to subdue Darl. Cash is surprised to see Dewey Dell scratching and beating Darl and to hear Jewel yelling, "Kill him. Kill the son of a bitch." When Cash realizes that Dewey Dell turned Darl in as the barn burner, he is perplexed. He had always believed that there was a strong bond between the two. Darl looks at Cash and says that he thought he would have told him what they had planned to do. He begins to laugh. Then, he becomes quiet and asks if Cash wants him to go. When Cash replies that it might be better for him, Darl starts laughing uncontrollably.

Peabody, annoyed at what the family has done to Cash's leg, tells him he will be lucky if he ever walks again. He says they could have fixed him better by sawing off his leg at the local mill. He warns Cash that he will have a limp, if he ever is able to walk again. Cash, stoic as ever, responds that it does not hurt much and that, as his father said, it is lucky he broke the same leg which was broken before.

Dewey Dell, in her best clothes, tries to find help from a Jefferson druggist. In the drugstore, she is fooled into thinking that the clerk is a doctor. MacGowan tells his friend, Jody, to watch out for the real druggist while he tries to wheedle Dewey Dell into having sex with him. MacGowan realizes she is inexperienced and naive. He gives her some innocuous mixture to drink and tells her to come back that night for the rest of the cure. In the evening, he

gives her some capsules filled with talcum powder and then tells her that to reverse the pregnancy she must have sex again. He leads her to the cellar for her "cure." On her way back to the hotel, Dewey Dell begins to realize she has been duped. She tells Vardaman, who has accompanied her, that they will have to slip back into their hotel so no one will notice that they were gone.

In his last narrative, Darl speaks of himself in the third person. He describes sitting on the train to Jackson, between the two attendants who have taken him away. Darl has become incoherent and either laughs or repeatedly mumbles aloud "Yes, yes, yes, ..."

After stealing Cash's eight dollars and selling Jewel's horse, Anse is still in need of money. Finding the ten dollars Lafe gave Dewey Dell for the abortion, he takes it from her. She tells him it is not hers to give. She says it belongs to Cora Tull, that it was loaned to her to buy something. Anse, crying ingratitude and misfortune, takes the money from Dewey Dell.

Before they return the borrowed spades, Jewel wants to take Cash to Peabody's. Anse wants to return the spades first. Jewel says he or Vardaman could do it quicker, but Anse wants to return them in person. When the spades are returned, Cash goes to the doctor. Anse says he has errands to run and returns clean-shaven and spruced up. He asks if there is any more money and tells them to wait at the corner for him. When he returns, he is carrying a suitcase and looks different to them. Then they realize that he has bought his teeth and is wearing them. He is accompanied by the "duck-shaped woman" with the "hard-looking pop eyes." It is her gramophone he carries. Cash thinks that Darl would have enjoyed the music. However, he knows that it is best for Darl to be in Jackson since "this world is not his world." The family is shocked when Anse introduces this woman as the new Mrs. Bundren.

Analysis

Darl's attempts to prevent the family from carrying Addie to Jefferson have failed. He tries to explain to Vardaman that Addie should rest in peace and, when he says she wishes to "lay down her life," Darl implies that she wants to die. He treats her as if she is still alive. When he and Vardaman listen to her moving and mumbling in her coffin, he tells Vardaman, "She's talking to God. She is calling on Him to help her." Darl appears to believe that Addie

needs to be saved. Returning to the gothic theme, it is as if she is possessed and that stopping the trip to Jefferson would somehow save her soul. He says to Vardaman that she wants to hide from the sight of man "so she can lay down her life." The theme of the vampire, desperate to return to rest in its own earth lest it die, is reflected here. If Darl can prevent Addie's burial in her family plot, she finally will be able to rest in peace, "lay down her life."

Darl does not try to help Jewel rescue Addie's coffin from the fire. It is obvious that he wants her to burn in the barn. Jewel knows this and risks his own life to get Addie out of the barn. When Jewel first enters the burning building, he stops at the coffin and Darl tells him to go save the horses. Jewel realizes that Darl knows the living animals will be everyone's first priority and glares at his brother. Darl is thwarted, however, when Jewel escapes his grasp and runs back into the barn to rescue Addie after all the animals have been saved. The unsuccessful Darl cries on the scorched casket while the uncomprehending Vardaman consoles him, "You needn't to cry. Jewel got her out. You needn't to cry Darl."

As Addie had indicated to Cora before her death, "He [Jewel] is my cross and he will be my salvation. He will save me from the water and from the fire. Even though I have laid down my life, he will save me." Addie's prophecy has come true. Darl, the child Cora says was "Touched by God Himself," has been defeated by Addie and Jewel. The child whose language refers to Hell and damnation has been the one to win his mother's soul for her. The child who was touched by God has lost his reason and has been condemned to live his life in an asylum.

In order to prevent Darl from telling what he knows about her, Dewey Dell has turned her brother in to the authorities for burning the Gillespie barn. Because people consider him strange anyway, the family arranges to have him taken to an asylum rather than a jail. Jewel, watching Dewey Dell and the officials wrestle Darl to the ground, shouts to them to kill Darl. It is as if Jewel wants to exact some personal revenge for the obstacles which Darl had presented along the journey. The conflict between the brothers has come to a head and Jewel has won. Darl, restrained by the authorities, is reduced to uncontrolled laughter or idiotic ramblings. His uncanny ability to see into people has left him. He can no longer recognize even himself, and he speaks of "Darl" as if he were a separate person.

Though the story has these highly tragic and horrific aspects, the dark comic potential of Anse cannot be overlooked. In many ways, Anse is similar to the kind of cartoon character who causes disaster wherever he goes, yet manages to come out of the situation unscathed. He is an exasperating, irritating, and annoyingly successful character.

Throughout the entire novel, Anse avoids pain, indignity, death, and sacrifice. His family members suffer death, mutilation, and physical and psychological pain. They surrender their money, their freedom, and their desires. They go through fires and floods. They do all this with little or no complaint. Anse, the chronic whiner, never lifts a finger to help, to work, to console, or to sweat. It is ironic that the man who said that working and sweating would make him die is able to accomplish so much in so little time once they get to Jefferson. They are there barely two days and Anse manages to get the money, the girl, and the teeth.

As I Lay Dying can be read a number of ways. Addie can be viewed as a malevolent force; or, she can be seen as one of the few admirable characters who are aware that deeds are more important than words. The novel is a tragedy, a comedy, a parable, a philosophical work, and a horror tale. It is no accident that it can fit so many interpretations. It follows Faulkner's multiple narrative pattern by providing many ways of looking for truth. It also demonstrates the difficulty of filtering through all that we see and hear in order to arrive at truth. The novel moves back and forth in time allowing many of the narratives to overlap at points. This provides us with different views of the same situation. However, it also confuses the timeline. Faulkner's novel is unsettling because it puts the reader off center. His jumbled historical (chronological) events, inaccurate language, and differing points of view are intentional. These are designed to raise questions, to make people think, and to indicate the difficulty in knowing what is true.

Study Questions

1. Who tries to stop Jewel from returning to the burning barn to save Addie?

2. What is Peabody's reaction when he sees Cash's leg in the cement cast?

3. What reactions does the wagon get as it approaches the town of Jefferson?

4. When Anse criticizes Darl's suggestion that they go to the hardware store to buy spades with which to dig Addie's grave, what does Darl reply?

5. What does Jewel suggest they do with Darl before the authorities come to get him?

6. How many days has it been between Addie's death and her burial?

7. Why was Cash surprised that Dewey Dell turned Darl in to the authorities?

8. What is Cash's response when Darl, restrained by the officials from Jackson, asks him, "Do you want me to go?"?

9. When Anse tries to take the ten dollars from Dewey Dell, to whom does she say the money belongs?

10. What is Cash's reaction upon being introduced to the new Mrs. Bundren?

Answers

1. Jewel shakes him off when Darl grasps at his arm and tells him not to go back in. When Gillespie tries to stop Jewel from going back into the barn, Jewel knocks him down.

2. Peabody is appalled by what Anse has done to Cash's leg. He tells Cash that Anse should have cured it by sticking it into the saw at the sawmill and said, "Then you all could have stuck his head into the saw and cured a whole family."

3. Cars slow down on the road to stare at the wagon. People who live in the cabins come out, white-eyed, to watch them pass. Some negroes on the road turn in disgust and outrage at the smell coming from the wagon. A white man, walking ahead of the negroes, nearly gets into a fight with Jewel for staring at the wagon. At the town square, heads turn with disgust as they pass by.

4. Anse says that it will cost money, to which Darl, sarcastically replies, "Do you begrudge her it?" He is echoing the line which Anse has used throughout the journey to Jefferson, "I wouldn't begrudge her it," to show Anse for the hypocrite that he is.

5. Jewel says they should "fix him." He says that they should tie Darl up so he does not set fire to the team and the wagon.

6. Darl says that it has been nine days since Addie Bundren has died.

7. Cash always believed that Dewey Dell liked Darl best of all her siblings. He was surprised she turned on Darl because they had seemed to have a special bond; they seemed, he says, to have "knowed things betwixt them."

8. Cash tells Darl that it will be better for him in Jackson, "Quiet, with none of the bothering."

9. Dewey Dell first says the money belongs to Cora Tull. It is the money she got for selling the cakes. When Anse confronts her as having had no cakes to sell, Dewey Dell then says the money was given to her to buy something for someone.

10. Cash envisions the family, including the new Mrs. Bundren, sitting around on winter nights, listening to the music of the latest record from the mail order on her gramophone. He says it is a shame Darl cannot be with them, but he is probably better off because "this world is not his world."

Suggested Essay Topics

1. Examine Darl's actions and speech in this last section of the novel. At what point does it seem that he is beginning to "crack up"? What are the indications?

2. What significant changes have occurred in Anse in the last section of the book? How do you account for these changes?

3. Cash has suffered silently throughout the last section of this novel. He rarely complains and the advice he offers is largely ignored. However, he is a level-headed and observant character. Though he does not protest very strongly about

the family's plans for Darl, Cash obviously thinks about the matter in great detail. Through a careful examination of his reactions, explain how Cash may be viewed as the most reasonable or realistic of the Bundrens.

4. By the time the family reaches Jefferson, Dewey Dell is desperate for a way to end her pregnancy and avoid having others find out about her condition. Examine her exchanges with MacGowan. Ho was Dewey Dell changed? Howw has this change affected her attitude toward Darl? Based on her experiences, what kind of person might she become?

SECTION SEVEN

Sample Analytical Paper Topics

The following paper topics are designed to test your under-standing of the novel as a whole and to analyze important themes and literary devices. Following each question is a sample outline to get you started.

Topic #1

Nature plays as vital a part in many stories and poems as the characters do. *As I Lay Dying* relies a great deal on Nature and her forces to move the story line along. What universal natural symbols does Faulkner rely on and how does he incorporate them into the action of the novel?

Outline

I. Thesis Statement: *The forces of Nature and the natural world compete against man in Faulkner's novel,* As I Lay Dying.

II. The Bundren homestead

    A. House built on a very steep hill

    B. Gravity and angles make house seem warped or mysterious

    C. Anse's view of the road in front of the Bundren house

III. The rainstorm

    A. Keeps people away from the house

    B. Makes travel from or to the Bundren house difficult

C. Accompanies or announces Addie's death

D. Causes bridges to be washed out

IV. The flooding river

A. Impedes crossing and slows the family down

B. Drenches Addie's corpse

C. Drowns mules

D. Causes Cash to break his leg and get kicked by the horse.

V. Hot weather

A. Adds to discomfort and short tempers

B. Causes decomposing body to decay and smell sooner

C. Helps attract cat and buzzards to the wagon

VI. Birth and death

A. Dewey Dell's view of birth/pregnancy

B. Addie's view of birth and children

C. Bundren children's relationship to Addie Bundren

D. Addie Bundren's view of death

E. Addie's family's view of death

VII. Conclusion: The Bundrens, an "unnatural" family, find every aspect of the natural world a challenge—whether it is birth, weather, geography, or death.

Topic #2

Addie Bundren maintains that words are not important; they go straight up and bear no relation to things that happen. Words are important for Faulkner, however. Examine the names and the descriptions of the characters. Paying careful attention to descriptive phrases, imagery, and adjectives, discuss whether or not Faulkner is successful in drawing his characters.

Outline

I.   Thesis Statement: *Faulkner selects his descriptive words and phrases carefully in order to help the reader create a better picture—both physically and psychologically—of the characters in* As I Lay Dying.

II. Dewey Dell

    A.   Double meanings in her name

    B.   Association with earth/land

    C.   Association with farm animals

    D.   Words used by MacGowan and Jody

    E.   Words used by Darl

III. Jewel

    A.   Why Addie gave him this name

    B.   Words Darl uses to describe him

    C.   Words Cora uses to describe him

    D.   Words Tull and Peabody use to describe him

    E.   Association with animals

IV. Darl

    A.   Meanings his name connotes

    B.   Words Anse uses to describe him

    C.   Words Cash uses to describe him

    D.   Words Cora uses to describe him

    E.   Words Tull and Peabody use to describe him

V.   Anse Bundren

    A.   Meanings his names connote

    B.   Association with animals

    C.   Words Addie uses to describe him

    D.   Words Darl uses to describe him

    E.   Words Peabody and Tull use to describe him

VI. Addie

    A. Meanings her name connotes

    B. Self-description and association with the dead/death

    C. Words Anse uses to describe her

    D. Words Cora uses to describe her

    E. Words Darl uses to describe her

VII. Conclusion: A reader can achieve a more complete under-standing of characters by examining how they appear to others in a story in addition to studying their own dialogue or narratives.

Topic #3

In *As I Lay Dying*, William Faulkner appears unhappy with how people understand or misunderstand and use or misuse their religion. Through a careful study of their narratives, consider what problems Faulkner might find inherent in religion and how those characters who express religious feeling should actually behave.

Outline

I. Thesis Statement: *Though a number of characters in the novel express belief in God, most of their religious feeling is misdirected or self-serving and falls short of being, what Cora Tull calls, "pure religious."*

II. Cora Tull

    A. Hymn singing

    B. Use of Bible quotes

    C. Her relationship/place with God, as she sees it

    D. Her view/opinion of others, in terms of her religion

    E. Her views on death/Great Unknown

    F. Her interpretation of our purpose in life

III. Anse Bundren

    A. How he interprets his place in God's eyes

    B. How he understands God's will

    C. His use of the Lord's name (when and how he uses it)

    D. His view of our purpose in life

IV. Whitfield

    A. What his role in the community is/has been

    B. How Cora Tull views his role

    C. How he views his role

    D. How Addie views him

    E. His sin or hypocrisy

V. Jewel

    A. His view of God

    B. His use of anti-religious language/terminology

VI. Dewey Dell

    A. Her motivation for believing in God

    B. Her view of what God does for people

    C. How she uses her church-going clothes

VII. Conclusion: Faulkner feels that religion is meaningless if its ultimate purpose is personal gain or it is empty if its teachings become mere words without human understanding.

Topic #4

Darl Bundren is a complex character who can be viewed as mysterious or menacing, sympathetic or deranged. Through a careful examination of Darl's narratives and those narratives which describe him, try to establish the "true" character of Darl.

Outline

I. Thesis Statement: *Though others consider Darl to be "strange," his narratives reveal that he is capable of a deeper understanding of himself and the people around him than are many of the other characters in the novel.*

II. Cora Tull's view of Darl

    A. Believes Darl has a "natural affection" for his mother

    B. Discusses the "understanding" between Darl and Addie

    C. Disagrees with others in the community who say that Darl is "queer"

III. Dewey Dell's view of Darl

    A. Knows he can communicate/know things without words

    B. Fears and hates Darl because of his uncanny ability

    C. Wants to kill Darl because she feels he "controls" their trip to Jefferson

IV. Anse's view of Darl

    A. Feels that Darl has been taken from him, is more interested in his own business and the land than in Anse

    B. Criticizes Darl for his peculiar fits of laughter

V. Vardaman's view of Darl

    A. Tries to understand Darl's explanation of the relationship between Addie and her sons and the Bundren brothers

    B. Is confused about Darl's inability to save Addie from the river, though Darl is a good "grabbler"

    C. Describes Darl's concern for Cash's health and Dewey Dell's "cakes"

    D. Describes "listening" to Addie with Darl at night; discusses the buzzards

    E. Seems to become obsessed with the fact that Darl has been taken to Jackson

VI. Cash's view of Darl

    A. Describes why the officials come for Darl

    B. Sympathizes with Darl's attempts to stop Addie's journey to Jefferson

    C. Discusses how Darl seemed to expect the officials, and how he and Dewey Dell "kind of knowed things betwixt them"

    D. Tries to ascertain why Darl burned the barn

    E. Explains why it might be better for Darl to go to the asylum in Jackson

    F. Regrets that Darl cannot be with the family

VII. Darl's view of the world

    A. His description of his childhood

    B. His relationship with Jewel, Dewey Dell, and Vardaman

    C. His descriptions of the Bundren house and its environment

    D. The significance of his italicized portions of the narrative

    E. His philosophical and introspective examinations of himself and others

VIII. Conclusion: Darl Bundren is a self-aware and sensitive character whose ability to understand the significance of people and events around him becomes a liability, sending him to the insane asylum and proving that "this world is not his world."

Topic #5

Although Addie Bundren says words have no meaning, William Faulkner's use of metaphors, similes, and figurative language, in *As I Lay Dying*, work to make his scenery, and his characters and their actions, more vivid. For example, he describes how Addie's eyes, when she is on her deathbed, look "like two candles when you watch them gutter down into the sockets of iron candlesticks." Examine the types of figurative language Faulkner uses in drawing either his scenery or one of his characters. Describe how figurative language makes these more intense and how it adds, overall, to the tone of his novel.

Outline

I.   Thesis Statement: *William Faulkner's use of figurative language adds to the vividness of character [or scenery] in his novel.*

II. Defining figurative and literal language

    A. Metaphor

    B. Simile

    C. Metonymy

    D. Synecdoche

    E. Personification

III. Figurative language used to describe a character's [scene's] appearance

    A. Menacing or negative language

    B. Natural versus unnatural language

    C. Animal imagery/personification

    D. Religious figurative language

IV. Figurative language used by the character under examination

    A. In describing other people

    B. In describing scenery or surroundings

    C. In describing animals

V.   Characters more [or less] prone to using figurative language

    A. Bundren family members

    B. Tulls

    C. Whitfield

    D. Other characters

VI. Figurative language as an extension of character [scene]

    A. Enhancing scenery or an exchange between characters

    B. Paralleling the action in a particular scene

VII. Conclusion: The extensive use of figurative language in *As I Lay Dying* helps the reader to understand the characters and the story by directing attention to the types and frequency of figurative language used.

Topic #6

Intimate relationships (husbands and wives, lovers) are among the most important because they are based on trust and respect and because they often produce children/offspring who will contribute to the development of the future. The way in which people treat these relationships influences others, especially children. In *As I Lay Dying*, Faulkner depicts a number of different types of intimate relationships. Describe the nature of these relationships and how they might affect the emotional and social growth of those young people who observe them.

Outline

I.   Thesis Statement: *The intimate relationships of adults often affect the way in which children, young people, and others view intimacy, love, and marriage and have an important impact on the socal development of children and young people.*

II. Married life of Addie and Anse Bundren

    A.   Courtship

    B.   Marriage

    C.   Home life

    D.   Attitudes towards their children

    E.   Attitudes towards intimacy and trust

    F.   Attitudes towards respect and promises

    G.   Attitudes towards one another

    H.   Attitudes towards family in terms of religious duty

III. Married life of Cora and Vernon Tull

    A.   Attitudes towards their children

    B.   Attitudes towards intimacy and trust

    C.   Attitudes towards respect and promises

    D.   Attitudes towards family duty and responsibility

    E.   Attitudes towards one another

    F.   Attitudes towards family in terms of religious duty

IV. Rachel and Samson
- A. Attitudes towards respect and promises
- B. Attitudes towards family duty and responsibility
- C. Attitudes towards one another

V. Armstid and Lula
- A. Attitudes towards respect and promises
- B. Attitudes towards family duty and responsibility
- C. Attitudes towards one another

VI. Dewey Dell and Lafe
- A. Attitudes towards respect and promises
- B. Attitudes towards family duty and responsibility
- C. Attitudes towards one another
- D. Attitudes towards their child
- E. Attitudes towards intimacy and trust

VII. Dewey Dell and MacGowan
- A. Attitudes towards respect and promises
- B. Attitudes towards responsibility
- C. Attitudes towards one another
- D. Attitudes towards intimacy and trust

VIII. Anse and the new Mrs. Bundren (the duck-shaped woman)
- A. Courtship
- B. Attitudes towards family/children

IX. The Bundren childrens' attitudes towards their parents' relationship
- A. How Darl views Anse's promises to Addie
- B. How Darl interprets his mother's position in the marriage
- C. How Jewel views Anse's promises to Addie
- D. Dewey Dell's inability to confide in either parent

    E.   Cash's view of Anse's promises to Addie

    F.   Vardaman's view of his parents

X.   How others view the relationship between Anse and Addie

    A.   Cora

    B.   Tull

    C.   Peabody

    D.   Whitfield

    E.   Samson and Rachel

    F.   Armstid and Lula

XI. Conclusion: The people whose relationships are depicted in *As I Lay Dying* feel angry, empty, cheated, warped/twisted, or unhappy and can only hurt the children's and young people's conceptions about closeness and intimacy.

Topic #7

Although many of his works contain distasteful, horrific, or "ugly" characters and situations, William Faulkner has been considered a writer with a strong sense of moral and religious values. These values do not adhere to the teachings of any one religion; they do share, however, a sense that any meaningful morality must be based in thoughtful and compassionate acts. Without compassion, mankind would find itself swept into chaos. This becomes clear when examining the characters in *As I Lay Dying*.

Outline

I.   Thesis Statement: *Several of the characters in William Faulkner's* As I Lay Dying *normally would be considered morally admirable by the rest of society; however, Faulkner makes it clear that we cannot "judge a book by its cover" and forces us to examine the true nature of what it is to be a "moral" person.*

II.   Anse

    A.   The typical role a father is expected to fill in a family

    B.   Anse as his family's financial support

     C. Anse as his family's emotional support

     D. Anse's concern for/attitude about his wife's death

     E. Anse's concern for/attitude about his children

     F. How Anse uses promises/sacred words to justify his actions

III. Whitfield

     A. The type of personality and insight a man in his occupation should have

     B. How he presents himself to his congregation

     C. What Cora thinks is the nature of his relationship with Addie

     D. How Addie first views their relationship

     E. What happens to Addie's and Whitfield's affair

     F. How he reflects on his relationship with Addie

IV. Cora Tull

     A. How she expresses herself in terms of her religion

     B. How she compares herself to other people

     C. Her accuracy in judging others

V. Moseley

     A. The type of personality a man in his occupation should have

     B. His judgment of Dewey Dell based on her appearance

     C. His reaction to her request

     D. His reaction to the information his assistant gives him about the Bundren family

VI. Peabody

     A. The type of personality and insight a man in his occupation should have

     B. His attitude towards Addie's death

     C. His attitude towards the Bundrens and the Tulls

     D. Dewey Dell's attitude towards Peabody

VII. Conclusion: In *As I Lay Dying*, Faulkner indicates that those whom we generally trust to be the most moral, trustworthy, sympathetic, and understanding lack the necessary understanding or compassion to help sustain others. Their outward appearances and actions often conceal selfishness, weaknesses, or inability to deal with problems in a meaningful way.

SECTION EIGHT

Bibliography

The following edition of the text was used in preparing this study guide:

Faulkner, William. *As I Lay Dying*. New York: Vintage Books, 1964.

More background on Faulkner's life, his literary style, and his themes can be found in the following works:

Cowley, Malcolm. *The Faulkner-Cowley File: Letters and Memories, 1944-1962*. New York: Penguin Books, 1978.

Jehlen, Myra. *Class and Character in Faulkner's South*. New York: Columbia University Press, 1976.

Oates, Stephen B. *William Faulkner: The Man and the Artist*. New York: Harper & Row Publishers, 1987.

Waggoner, Hyatt H. *William Faulkner: From Jefferson to the World*. Lexington: University of Kentucky Press, 1966.

REA's **Test Preps**
The Best in Test Preparation

- REA "Test Preps" are far **more** comprehensive than any other test preparation series
- Each book contains up to **eight** full-length practice exams based on the most recent exams
- **Every** type of question likely to be given on the exams is included
- Answers are accompanied by **full** and **detailed** explanations

REA has published over 60 Test Preparation volumes in several series. They include:

Advanced Placement Exams (APs)
Biology
Calculus AB & Calculus BC
Chemistry
Computer Science
English Language & Composition
English Literature & Composition
European History
Government & Politics
Physics
Psychology
Spanish Language
United States History

College Level Examination Program (CLEP)
American History I
Analysis & Interpretation of Literature
College Algebra
Freshman College Composition
General Examinations
Human Growth and Development
Introductory Sociology
Principles of Marketing

SAT II: Subject Tests
American History
Biology
Chemistry
French
German
Literature

SAT II: Subject Tests (continued)
Mathematics Level IC, IIC
Physics
Spanish
Writing

Graduate Record Exams (GREs)
Biology
Chemistry
Computer Science
Economics
Engineering
General
History
Literature in English
Mathematics
Physics
Political Science
Psychology
Sociology

ACT - American College Testing Assessment

ASVAB - Armed Service Vocational Aptitude Battery

CBEST - California Basic Educational Skills Test

CDL - Commercial Driver's License Exam

CLAST - College Level Academic Skills Test

ELM - Entry Level Mathematics

ExCET - Exam for Certification of Educators in Texas

FE (EIT) - Fundamentals of Engineering Exam

FE Review - Fundamentals of Engineering Review

GED - High School Equivalency Diploma Exam (US & Canadian editions)

GMAT - Graduate Management Admission Test

LSAT - Law School Admission Test

MAT - Miller Analogies Test

MCAT - Medical College Admission Test

MSAT - Multiple Subjects Assessment for Teachers

NTE - National Teachers Exam

PPST - Pre-Professional Skills Tests

PSAT - Preliminary Scholastic Assessment Test

SAT I - Reasoning Test

SAT I - Quick Study & Review

TASP - Texas Academic Skills Program

TOEFL - Test of English as a Foreign Language

RESEARCH & EDUCATION ASSOCIATION
61 Ethel Road W. • Piscataway, New Jersey 08854
Phone: (908) 819-8880

Please send me more information about your Test Prep Books

Name _____

Address _____

City _____ State _____ Zip _____

Available at your local bookstore or order directly from us by sending in coupon below.

MAXnotes®

REA's Literature Study Guides

MAXnotes® are student-friendly. They offer a fresh look at masterpieces of literature, presented in a lively and interesting fashion. **MAXnotes®** offer the essentials of what you should know about the work, including outlines, explanations and discussions of the plot, character lists, analyses, and historical context. **MAXnotes®** are designed to help you think independently about literary works by raising various issues and thought-provoking ideas and questions. Written by literary experts who currently teach the subject, **MAXnotes®** enhance your understanding and enjoyment of the work.

Available **MAXnotes®** include the following:

Absalom, Absalom!
The Aeneid of Virgil
Animal Farm
Antony and Cleopatra
As I Lay Dying
As You Like It
The Autobiography of
    Malcolm X
The Awakening
Beloved
Beowulf
Billy Budd
The Bluest Eye, A Novel
Brave New World
The Canterbury Tales
The Catcher in the Rye
The Color Purple
The Crucible
Death in Venice
Death of a Salesman
The Divine Comedy I: Inferno
Dubliners
Emma
Euripedes' Electra & Medea
Frankenstein
Gone with the Wind
The Grapes of Wrath
Great Expectations
The Great Gatsby
Gulliver's Travels
Hamlet
Hard Times

Heart of Darkness
Henry IV, Part I
Henry V
The House on Mango Street
Huckleberry Finn
I Know Why the Caged
    Bird Sings
The Iliad
Invisible Man
Jane Eyre
Jazz
The Joy Luck Club
Jude the Obscure
Julius Caesar
King Lear
Les Misérables
Lord of the Flies
Macbeth
The Merchant of Venice
The Metamorphoses of Ovid
The Metamorphosis
Middlemarch
A Midsummer Night's Dream
Moby-Dick
Moll Flanders
Mrs. Dalloway
Much Ado About Nothing
My Antonia
Native Son
1984
The Odyssey
Oedipus Trilogy

Of Mice and Men
On the Road
Othello
Paradise Lost
A Passage to India
Plato's Republic
Portrait of a Lady
A Portrait of the Artist
    as a Young Man
Pride and Prejudice
A Raisin in the Sun
Richard II
Romeo and Juliet
The Scarlet Letter
Sir Gawain and the
    Green Knight
Slaughterhouse-Five
Song of Solomon
The Sound and the Fury
The Stranger
The Sun Also Rises
A Tale of Two Cities
Taming of the Shrew
The Tempest
Tess of the D'Urbervilles
Their Eyes Were Watching God
To Kill a Mockingbird
To the Lighthouse
Twelfth Night
Uncle Tom's Cabin
Waiting for Godot
Wuthering Heights

RESEARCH & EDUCATION ASSOCIATION
61 Ethel Road W. • Piscataway, New Jersey 08854
Phone: (908) 819-8880

Please send me more information about MAXnotes®.

Name _____

Address _____

City _____ State _____ Zip _____